Homesick for the Hills

Homesick for the Hills

By

Alyce Faye Bragg

Mountain State Press
Charleston, West Virginia

Some essays have been published in the weekday morning or Sunday editions of *The Charleston Gazette*, Charleston, West Virginia, *The Clay Herald*, Clay, West Virginia, or *The Clay County Free Press*, Clay, West Virginia between June 16, 1982 and May 14, 1997.

International Standard Book Number: 0-941092-41-0

Library of Congress Catalog Card Number: 99-075472

Mountain State Press
c/o The University of Charleston
2300 MacCorkle Avenue, S.E.
Charleston, WV 25304

Printed in the United States of America

This is a Mountain State Press book produced in affiliation with the University of Charleston, Charleston, West Virginia. Mountain State Press is solely responsible for editorial decisions.

About the Author

Alyce Faye Bragg still resides at Ovapa with her husband Criss. In addition to their six children, they now have a total of twenty grandchildren and two great-grandchildren. She not only writes about the country life, she also lives it.

OTHER BOOKS BY
ALYCE FAYE BRAGG

"THIS HOLLER IS MY HOME"

The book cover was painted by Mary Ellen Friend; sister of the author. It depicts the family home place of their childhood, with Pilot Knob in the background. Mary Ellen and her husband, Howard, reside at Ravenswood, West Virginia.

Dedicated to my long-suffering husband Criss, who sat alone many nights on the porch swing while I typed. Special thanks to my grandson Jeremy for his computer help and to my loving family who provides the material for my writing.

TABLE OF CONTENTS

PROLOGUE

"Going back home,"——a phrase that strikes a nostalgic note in the heart of almost everyone who goes away from home. The hills of Appalachia seem to have a stronger hold on the folks who populate its hollers and ridges.

Although many of its people have left its hills and migrated to other states and other life styles, still there is a longing in the heart to go back home.

Home may have been an old Jenny Lind house nestled up one of its innumerable hollers, with rough, un-painted boards on the outside and papered inside with heavy gray or blue Wallrite wallpaper. It could have been perched high on a mountain ridge, where the wind sighed through the trees and whipped icy winter blasts through the eaves.

Many homes were hidden in mountain coves, where deep woods almost obscured them. Reached only by a footpath, they were isolated from the world and a sanctuary to those families who dwelt there. Home could have been a dwelling place along the Elk River, where the waters lulled one to sleep with its rippling, liquid sound.

In times past, most of them were built with a little path out back that led to the "outhouse" or toilet, which served as a bathroom. It wasn't really a bathroom of course, as bathing was generally done in a No. 3 zinc washtub. Water for drinking and cooking was dipped from a cold mountain spring, or carried in buckets from a hand-powered pitcher pump.

Some had drilled wells equipped with a tube-like baler fastened to a rope, which was wound up on a windlass. Laundry was sometimes done in rainwater that poured off the roof into barrels or washtubs, or was carried from creeks or rivers in buckets. The washboard and lye soap were essential supplies for washday and elbow grease was supplied by the country housewife.

The house was surrounded by out-buildings, all necessary to country life. The barn, many times built of hewed logs, housed the livestock and also contained hay for wintertime feeding. There was generally a smoke-house, where hams and sides of bacon were cured and smoked, then hung from the rafters.

A cellar was usually dug out in a bank, where its coolness kept the jars and churns of sauerkraut, pickled beans and corn, and root vegetables through-out the winter.

Every farm had a big garden, where vegetables were raised for summertime usage and preserved for winter's need, plus a huge patch of field corn for meal, hominy and livestock feeding. Fruit trees provided apples, cherries,

and plums. A flock of chickens supplied
the family with fresh eggs and meat,
with the surplus eggs traded to the
general store for salt and sugar and
other items that couldn't be raised.
These little country farms were almost
self-sufficient.

Most of them are gone now. Many of
them have been sold, the buildings
razed and modern dwellings built instead. Some of them have been simply
abandoned, leaving the house to fall
away into decay, slowly reverting back
to the soil. An old vacant farm is a
sad sight

The barn and outbuildings collapse
in a heap, the yard that displayed
hollyhocks and rambler roses is over-
grown with weeds and underbrush and
gardens and fields lie fallow. Trees
spring up where corn and vegetables
once grew. The land looks forsaken.

There is not a trace of the family
who once lived there, experienced joys
and sorrows, births and deaths. Only
memories linger.

Although the home place may be
gone and the folks who lived there
scattered to other places and other
life styles, those who have their roots
anchored in the hills feel a longing to
go home again.

In memory, we walk once again
through the wooded hills, splash barefoot in the mountain streams and pick
wild flowers and mountain teaberries
that grow on the hillsides. We dip a

tin cup into a pure, clear spring and drink deeply of its satisfying water.

We plunge again in the old swimming hole, its cool water so welcome after a hard day of hoeing corn. The porch swing holds family members, some of them long gone, who sit and listen to the sweet, piercing call of the whippoorwill.

Memories are a blessing, for through them we can always go back home...

INTRODUCTION

Ovapa is a small community, actually a wide place in the road. It has been my home for over 64 years now, with my great-grandchildren making seven generations of the same family living on the old home place.

We still live much as our grandparents did, raising our gardens, canning and preserving the surplus, with our lives centered around church, family and home.

The men in the family keep their hunting dogs, and bring home the wild game that our forefathers hunted and used. It is a peaceful, serene life on the whole, with time to sit on the porch swing at night and listen to the whippoorwills and tree frogs.

This selection of columns will take you back to yesterday, to a more gentle, slower way of life. It may not have been better, but it seemed that way.

I have been reading with interest the study on Appalachia made by a group of our finest minds attempting to define where it is and what it is. While I would never presume to align my simple mind with these intellectual thinkers and learned scholars, I know what Appalachia means to me.

My dictionary states baldly that it is a region in the Eastern United States, covering parts of eleven states, with a population of fifteen million, regarded as an area of wide-spread poverty and unemployment. Perhaps these are the bare facts, but Appalachia is more, so much more.

Appalachia means clear mountain springs, bordered by moss and ferns, where cold, refreshing water is scooped up in a tin cup. Drinking from one of these springs is assurance that a person will always return to the hills.

It is the hills in their many moods, from the swelling buds of springtime to the full, lush growth of summer; from the unmatched splendor of fall foliage to the stark, bare beauty of winter. It's the path through the deep woods, past rhododendron thickets, across fast-running rivulets, to the crest of the mountain where the hills and valleys fold and unfold as far as the eye can see. It's the swift-flowing rivers that rush onward toward immense boulders, to leap and foam as they sing their mountain song.

Appalachia has been populated for generations by honest and hard-working folk, who say just what they mean and mean what they say. There are plenty of neighbors here in the hills whose word is their bond and you can depend completely upon what they tell you.

Faith has not died out in Appalachia, for there are Godfearing and dedicated families who live by the Word of God and are raising their children to live by the same. The outside world may call us fanatics, but we have peace of mind and contentment unknown by unbelievers.

It is walking the same land that our fathers, grandfathers and great-grandfathers walked. Their proud and independent spirits speak to us from the earth, nurturing a love for the soil that is passed down through the generations.

I feel my grandmother's presence when I work in the same garden that she tended, dropping the seeds carefully from my apron pocket in the same manner that she did. I see her down through the years, as she was long ago, her gold-rimmed spectacles perched on the end of her nose and sunbonnet shading her eyes from the sun.

She has on the voluminous white apron that she always wore, each side grimed in garden dirt where she wiped her hands as she worked. It seems that I can feel her approval as I take joy in the task of gardening.

It is embodied in the old hand-whittled shucking peg, banded by a circle of leather and worn smooth by years of hard work. It speaks now of backbreaking fields of corn, plowed by horse and double-shovel plow and hoed by hand during days of long, hot toil in the burning sun. It is a true symbol of earning your bread by the sweat of your brow.

Appalachia is graveyards (not cemeteries) high on windswept mountaintops where we bury our dead, so that when the last trumpet sounds and the graves burst open, they will be that much nearer heaven. Families gather there on Decoration (Memorial) Day to clean off the graves and decorate them with fresh flowers. Many family reunions are held at that time, where family ties are strengthened as the older folk visit together and the younger ones run and play.

Many of our people have had to leave Appalachia and seek employment in other states across the country. Yet they seem to leave a part of themselves behind that must be satisfied from time to time by family reunions. Back they come to the hills, back to the old home place, to reaffirm their roots and store courage to venture out into the world again. Appalachia is that longing in the heart to come home again.

Chapter 1

SNOWY DAYS IN THE HILLS

"Let him push at the door —in the
chimney roar,
And rattle at the windowpane;
Let him in at us spy with his
icicle eye
But he shall not entrance gain."
...Thomas Noel

On the wings of a cold north wind, winter weather was carried into our hills last night, sending bird and wild creature alike scurrying for shelter. The brown landscape is coated with an icy, white coating and while the creek is still running, the edges are beginning to freeze along the banks. Overhanging twigs create ice bells that dangle in the water and mild winter days are now a memory.

The grandkids look forward to a genuine cold spell, when the schools are closed and there is enough snow to ride their sleighs. Bundled up in their snowsuits, mittens, and boots, they revel in their freedom until cold drives them in. Shedding outerwear as they troop through the door, they soon have the Monopoly board spread underfoot and cookies and hot chocolate passed around. Some things never change and Monopoly has been a staple in our home ever since I can remember. Gone are the days when I exulted in "snow piled wide and deep," although (and wipe that pained expression off your faces, grandchildren) winters when I was a kid were much colder and the snows were deeper and more frequent. I can still remember the excitement when a deep snow began to fall.

Dragging out sleighs with steel runners, bulky, homemade sleds that were almost too heavy to pull, or pieces of linoleum when we had neither sleigh nor sled, we would head for the nearest hill. The cold didn't seem to bother us much; we would wipe a grimy coat sleeve across a runny nose and take another dive downhill.

We used to keep a pasteboard box of caps, gloves, toboggans and mittens beside the door for wintertime use. When we couldn't find mittens, we would wear old socks on our hands. Boots for girls weren't manufactured then as they are now, so we wore galoshes that fit over our shoes and snapped with two snaps. They didn't come up nearly far enough on our legs and the deeper snow would pack down in the top of our boots. The mark of wintertime among us girls was the wide band of red, chapped skin around our legs. Cloverine salve was the remedy for that.

Sleigh riding at Hagar School will never be forgotten. We used the path down the hill for a runway but the biggest thrill was the hump on the hill behind the Methodist Church. We called it "jumping the hump," and a sleigh going at top speed would shoot out six or eight feet in the air before it connected with the ground again.

Remember those snowball fights? We sometimes organized teams and staged a daylong battle. Ice balls (snowballs soaked in water and frozen) were outlawed; as well as foreign objects (rocks, etc.) imbedded in the snowball. It was a great joke to stuff a snowball down the back of someone's coat and run, fast.

The boys often got too rough, so we girls would wander off to make snow angels. We would find a patch of untouched snow, lie down on our backs and move our arms up and down to create wings.

When the snow was the right texture to pack easily, we made gigantic snowmen. Often we would roll the snow into such huge balls that it took three or four of us to lift one on top of the other. We played endless games of "fox and geese," treading out circles in the snow.

We would play until our hands and feet were almost frostbitten and our cheeks and noses reddened by the cold. How welcome was the call when Mom rounded us up for dinner! We would pile our wet coats, boots, gloves, and socks in front of the gas stove, where they soon emitted the peculiar steamy smell of wet wool.

Mom usually had a big pot of homemade vegetable soup ready to dish out and there was nothing as good in the world. (Even today, when we get our first real cold weather, I drag out the soup cooker. Thank goodness there is still enough family around to help eat it. It is impossible to make a small cooker of soup (it grows and grows).

As I watch my grandchildren play in the snow, it reminds me of the bobsled that "Preach" Bullard made one year. We had a beautiful, deep snowstorm that closed the schools and we took advantage of the unexpected holiday to play in the snow. We didn't have a lot of fancy sleighs that children have nowadays, so we would slide on anything we could find.

We looked out and saw Preach coming with a box-like contraption trailing behind him. When he reached our yard, he was grinning from ear to ear. He told us, "I've made a sled big enough for all of us to ride on."

It was big. Despite all our efforts, pushing and pulling, we couldn't get it more than three or four feet up the hill.. Dejected, Preach turned around and pulled his sleigh back down the road to his house. I wonder whatever happened to it. It would have made an excellent bomb shelter or a launching pad for a rocket to the moon. One thing for sure, it is undoubtedly still around. Something that sturdy is almost indestructible.

Sleds, soup, and Monopoly—they'll never be outdated.

The Charleston Gazette
January 24, 1992

We awaken to a silent white world this morning. Snow covers the hills and valleys, and outlines the starkly black limbs of the trees with a finger of white. The tall pine trees on the bank bow deeply under their burden of snow, while the graceful hemlocks at the edge of the yard are draped in Christmas card perfection. The leaden sky peers sullenly down upon this black and white world, where the only sound is the muttering of the creek as it makes its way between snow-covered banks.

The only evidence of yesterday's frivolity is the trampled yard marked by a multitude of booted footprints. The first significant snowfall of the year was greeted with cries of glee from the grandchildren (and some of their parents). The snow kept falling steadily, inviting the young and young in heart to play.

I watched out the window as booted, mittened and muffled to the eyebrows, they romped and played. The smaller boys frisked like puppies though the deepening snow, jumping and rolling in it. They carried huge icicles around that they had broken from the rock cliff bordering the yard, for what purpose only they knew. The little girls lay on their backs and made prim snow angels, ignoring the little boys. ' Soon their mothers organized a sleigh riding party, and off they trouped with their assorted gear to ride down a hill.

I was left to mind the kettle of soup, thinking how nice it was that I wasn't expected to join the revelers in the snow and could stay toasty warm beside the stove. Soon they will seek the sanctuary of the house, to devour bowls of soup with a chunk of hot batter bread baked in an iron skillet.

After awhile, I realize that I am not alone. One of the grandchildren, Luke, has stayed behind. "Don't you want to go sleigh riding?" I ask him. "Nope," he answers cheerfully. "I'm writing a story."

We all agree that Luke is "different." He is content to play alone for hours, while the rest of the grandchildren play in a group. When he does talk, his words come out in a tumbled rush.

He continues, "It's about a mother field mouse who has six children and lives in a brick—" "You mean a brick house?" I question. "No-no, Mommaw," he explains patiently. "It's a brick, like in a brick building, with holes in it. It's in a garden, and then she hears that the farmer is going to plow up the garden and she has to find another home for her babies and—" he pauses for breath.

(Sounds suspiciously like something I've heard.) "That's good, Lukie," I encourage him. "Why don't you type it?" For the next hour or so all I hear is the slow pecking of the typewriter keys as he labors over his story. He hands it to me with a generous, "You can use it in the paper if you want to."

He spies a clear plastic container and requests it for his "spider collection." Crystal, who has a paranoid fear of spiders, stumbled onto it when she visited them last weekend. I am afraid the three boys teased her unmercifully when they discovered that she responded so satisfactorily with screams and screeches.

Luke likes spiders. He explained to me quite reasonably about their life style and habits. How much of this was fact and how much fantasy, I don't know. When I asked him what they eat, he informed me that they eat bugs and flies. "Sometimes they suck the insides out and leave a hull," he explained. He told me a lot of things about spiders that I didn't know and a lot that I didn't care to know.

He made a foray out in the wash house and caught a couple of small spiders, which he put in the plastic container. Then he crumpled a couple of tissues in the box "so they can spin webs on it" he told me. Taking a needle, he punched a couple of holes in the lid. In spite of myself, I was becoming fascinated.

"That's air holes," he said in answer to my unspoken question. "And you have to take the lid off once in awhile to see about them, or they get bored and poke their little hands out of the air holes—"

I interrupted him, "Spiders have hands?"

"Sure," he answered with infinite patience at my ignorance. "That's what they have on the ends of their little arms. And they lay eggs and have lots of little babies . . ."

He ate his supper with his spider collection at his elbow, which he watched anxiously. After he went to bed, I checked the box to make sure the lid was on securely. I have a feeling, though, that it is going to be hard for me to carelessly smash a spider again. I keep seeing all those little hands waving in the air.

It is another snowy day, and I hear the grandchildren getting out of bed. I wonder what strange adventure awaits their grandmother this day. Think of the things we wouldn't learn if we didn't have grandchildren.

The Clay Herald
December 11, 1989

The snow crunches crisply underfoot and sparkles like diamonds as it reflects the gleam of the flashlight. The plank across the creek is treacherous with ice and snow, and the water runs swift and cold beneath.

As I shut the door of the chicken house, I can hear the soft clucking of the hens as they settle down for the night. I remember how astonished they acted this morning when I turned them out to a white, unfamiliar world. They quarreled querulously among themselves, lifting dainty feet to stand one-legged in the cold, unfamiliar, white stuff.

I hurry back to the house, fingers tingling and cheeks red with cold. As I creep gingerly across our ice-encrusted driveway, I reflect momentarily that there must be an easier life than winter in these hills.

It makes me think of a letter that I received from Mrs. Ruby Woods of Sebring, Ohio. There was a note of homesickness evident in her letter as she wrote,

"We hope your love affair with the hills and its people never dies. I was born at Dink, now called Rush Run Road. My mother spent all her youth in that holler, as did her mother and grandmother before her. My dad's family was originally from Virginia, but they found the lure of the hills irresistible. My granddad moved to Clendenin, then to Spencer and finally to the same holler and home place of my mother. My husband is also a Clay Countian, so my roots are deep in Clay County soil. So you see, the paper and your column is like a letter from home.

"When you speak of the hills, I again picture the hills, banks, flats, and valleys of our own home place on Rush. I dearly miss the smell of wood smoke on the crisp winter air—as I remember the feel of the heat from the old potbelly stove when you run back indoors. No gas stove or furnace can compare with this heat and the fragrance.

"So many of the things that the folks back home take for granted and don't fully enjoy hold such a dear place in my heart and memory. I pray for God's divine will to be done in our lives, but—in the yearnings of my heart, I'd like to be back home again.

"My personal picture of heaven here on earth is to have a pot of pinto beans on the back of the woodstove, slowly simmering in fresh spring water, hot sour dough biscuits in the oven and good friends sitting in our parlor—back home. To be back home! The hills and hollers of Clay County! I know so many Clay Countains, who for work or family reasons, have to live away from the hills, but they still feel as I do. Weekly you help to bring a piece of home to us."

My daughter Patty read her letter and exclaimed, "Mommy, you are making this lady so homesick. How come you write about the good things and don't say anything about the bad side? Why don't you write about the chapped, bleeding hands you get from carrying in the firewood (which produces the fragrant woodsmoke) or driving on narrow, winding roads covered with ice and snow?"

I guess she is right—I do emphasize the beauty of our state and sometimes it is a raw, primitive beauty. I admire the sturdy hillfolk who cling tenaciously to these rocky hillsides to carve out a meager living. There is a certain satisfaction in making it through another winter in order to plow again the same fields that our fathers and grandfathers plowed before us.

It is worth struggling through a hard winter to see spring burst forth in our hills. Winter doesn't last that long anyway. Next month brings Groundhog Day, and spring seems close at hand.

I heard a songbird outside my bedroom window this morning, singing a cheery song of spring. As I listened, I could almost hear phrases like "bursting buds on the lilac bush," "patches of violets under the apple tree," and "bird nests in the towering beeches." He, too, is looking forward to spring.

Our six-year-old grandson, David, has formed a singing group with the boys in the first grade (This helps pass a long winter). He said all except two boys were included. Mike was all primed to give him a lecture on discrimination, when he explained that he ran out of cards. "Membership cards," he explained patiently.

They are called the "Howling Foxes," and have an original song composed by Brian Legg (David says that Brian is the brains of the group). I didn't catch all the lyrics, but they included, "We like peanut butter, we like cars, but most of all we like you." The ending is sort of a yodel "youooooo-o-o-o." David says that Brian does the ending, because "He is the best howler that we have."

It must be sort of a club, because no girls are allowed. Benji's mother found a cryptic note in his pocket that read, "Everyday but Saturday." We think it is in code, but we haven't cracked it yet. She did find out that David had invited all the boys to his house on Saturday for a day of practice.

He sounds so much like his father, Mike. When he was in the third grade at Hagar School, his teacher called me and inquired, "Did you know anything about the note that Mike stuck up on the bulletin board?" I didn't. It read, "All boys interested in forming a Boy Scout Club meet at my house Saturday from 7 AM until 6 PM."

And people wonder what kids do for fun in winter in the country.

The Clay County Free Press
January 16, 1985

Winter woods . . .I have always loved them . . .

Pilot Knob glows like an amethyst in the last slanting rays of the

setting sun, the whole mountain bathed
in soft lavender color . . . the hills
seem to be waiting for the cold arms of
winter . . . even the woods have a
hushed, expectant look.

Winter woods have an austere
beauty all their own . . . we roamed
the hills and woods when we were kids .
. . winter and summer . . .only below-
zero temperatures kept us indoors . .
.these mild winter days set me
remembering . . . when the pale, wintry
sun would shine on fields of broomsage,
highlighting the golden wheat color. .
. and the dry, whispery rustle of the
stalks as we ran through the clumps
playing hide-and-seek . . . how the
wind would blow through the field,
moving the broomsage in undulating
waves.

We took to the woods in winter . .
. crossing the creek at the big rock
and winding our way uphill . . . the
ground underfoot would be wet and
spongy with its mat of thick leaves and
rich humus . . . patches of moss shone
bright green, and decaying logs covered
with a thick green coating . . . trees
stark and bare, with scrubby pines
standing out here and there . . .

We would stop and examine a bird
nest . . . knowing the birds had long
flown, but curious all the same . . .
sometimes there would be the fragment
of an eggshell . . . we marveled at the
workmanship of the nest ... sometimes

with horse hair wound neatly round and
round.

The woods were not bare and
deserted . . . we would catch the
glimpse of a big-eyed field mouse . . .
scurrying across our path to disappear
in a hole . . . an indignant chipmunk
perched on a stump, his tail jerking
furiously . . .loudly chirking in no
uncertain terms that we were on his
territory . . . we would examine the
animal tracks closely . . . thrilled
when we discovered a "big" deer track .
. . which was probably where the milk
cow slipped in the soft mud.

Single file, we tried to walk like
Indians in the woods . . . carefully
avoiding the dry sticks and crunchy
leaves . . . watching fearfully lest
some half-naked savage step out from
behind a tree with his tomahawk poised
to strike . . . the woods were
thrilling, even in winter.

Country kids are at home in the
woods . . . we could identify the sweet
birch twigs by their spotted bark,
although the leaves were gone . . . we
would break off and chew these
flavorsome tidbits . . . along with the
pungent spicewood bark . . . and last
year's mountain tea leaves, edged with
brown . . . tough and slightly bitter .
. . we ate it all . . . tasting even
the heart-shaped leaf we called
coltsfoot . . . dark, glossy green
leaves veined with darker green,
growing low on the ground . . . I can

still taste the bitter, "mediciney" flavor . . . nothing seemed to hurt us.

The pine thickets were my favorite place to play . . . branches thick-laced to form a cozy hideaway for children . . . the sun would coax the entrancing, resinous fragrance into the air . . . dry, brown needles forming a carpet underneath . . .

Sometimes there would be little pockets of unmelted snow deep in these thickets where the sun couldn't reach . . . the pine groves spoke to me of mysterious things . . . private worlds . . . delicious secrets . . . and they still do.

I could go back into these winter woods again . . . these same woods . . . I could cross the creek at the big rock . . . although the rock looks so much smaller, and the creek is different . . . I could climb the brown, leaf-covered hill . . . find winter—blasted mountain tea leaves, coltsfoot, and sweet birch bark . . . I could disappear into the fragrant pine grove . . . feel its mystery reach out to surround me as of old.

But I cannot enter into that long-ago world inhabited only by children and barred to adults forevermore. . . sometimes I get a glimpse of the other side. . . and memories abound.

But, oh, there are times when I wish I could go back!

The Charleston Gazette
January 17, 1992

Soft, feathery flakes of snow drift lazily down upon a world already clothed in winter white. Our hills are shivering under another siege of January weather, with the threat of even colder weather to come. Already the wind is picking up, flinging great clouds of snow in a swirling, macabre dance. It howls and shrieks around the eaves of the house like a demented soul, seeking a crevice or vulnerable spot to enter with its icy breath. It seems bent on snuffing out the life-giving warmth within.

On the sheer rock cliffs, the ice flows down in cascading ripples, while huge, jagged icicles hang down from the rocky ledges. The Arctic Clipper sails our hills tonight with full speed ahead.

We are snug and warm in our winter dens, and safe from the howling wind outside. We feed great chunks of wood to the woodstove, and it responds with glowing, cheery heat. The basic needs of food, clothing and shelter become more important now as we are cut off

25

more and more from the outside world. There is security in the woodpile, satisfaction in the cellar filled with canned goods and potatoes stashed in the bin.

We could survive until spring with the freezer stocked with food put away over the summer and with the rows of glass jars full of the garden's abundance. We might not have all the variety that we want, but we have all that we need. And that is just what the good Lord promised us, that He would supply all our need.

Today the chill factor hovers somewhere between 35° and 40° below zero and our normal, everyday routine, grinds to a halt. Church services are canceled and no traffic moves on the snow-covered road. Some of the most rewarding times we have enjoyed as a family have been during these winter storms that coop us up together

We dig out the Scrabble game or checker set, pop some corn, and bake some cookies. This is a good time to experiment with a new recipe or let novice cooks try their hands at preparing a meal. Crystal put together a fine pot of spaghetti one day last week when school was canceled and even the young grandchildren got into the spirit of it.

There's not too much to do except cook and eat but I wonder if boredom was a factor in Crystal's latest escapade. She found a magazine article on using natural ingredients to beautify your hair, so she decided to experiment. Her father came in the kitchen while she was brewing rosemary to make a rinse for her hair and asked curiously, "What smells like pork sausage?" I will admit that it did make her hair shiny and soft, so flushed with success, she decided to practice on someone else.

It just so happened that our pastor's daughter, Shelley, was spending the night with Crystal, as her parents were out of state attending a funeral. Shelley has very long hair, quite curly and almost black in color. She was led like a lamb to the slaughter.

The beauty article gave a remedy for frizzy hair (Shelley's hair is really not frizzy). It sounded a little odd to me. "Mix flour and water to make a smooth paste," the article read, "and apply liberally to the hair." It went on to say that flour was an ancient ingredient that makes the hair shaft lie flat.

It was church night, so the girls started early in order to have plenty of time. After a lengthy stay in the bathroom, they went on upstairs while we got ready for church. The first inkling I had of trouble was when Natalie, Shelley's little sister, came downstairs about twenty minutes before service time and announced in solemn tones, "I have seen messes in my life, but I don't think I've ever seen anything to compare to that one. They had left the flour-water paste on for twenty minutes, as the article directed, then attempted to comb it out. They rinsed and rinsed, but still it stuck. Desperate, they blow-dried it and tried to comb it out. The heat of the blow dryer had baked the dough in her hair until it hung down like long lasagna noodles. They had combed out a little fraction of it, along with a lot of hair. They had both been crying.

I told them they would have to wash it again, as we were going on to church. It looked as if it was going to be a long, drawn-out process. When we left, Shelley was bent over the bathtub and Crystal was in it working on her hair.

I called my sister Jeannie, who is part hairdresser and part nurse. She was properly sympathetic, but admitted that she had never encountered this problem before. As soon as we arrived at church, she asked me if they had gotten it out and I had to tell her honestly that I didn't think they'd ever get it out.

She came off the hill to try to assist them and found Shelley groaning in pain and despair and hoping desperately that her parents wouldn't return and find her in such a fix. She told Crystal grimly that it was a good thing that she loved her and they both bribed and threatened Natalie not to tell.

"That's no good, Shelley," Crystal told her. "If we don't tell them, they'll read it in the paper." After half a box of baking soda, and several applications of shampoo and cream rinse, Jeannie got most of it out. I'll have to say that Shelley really didn't look like Bess the landlord's daughter, plaiting a love knot in her long, black hair. But with some tomato sauce and cheese, she would have been mighty tasty.

We've closed down Crystal's beauty and noodle shop.

The Clay County Free Press
January 23, 1985

The snow sparkles like diamonds in the brilliant sunshine today, a welcome change from the days of continued snowfall. The air is cold and crisply invigorating, while the pines on the hill are bowed low under their burden of snow. Our last snow was one worthy of grandpa's day and one that will live in our memories for a long time.

The weatherman had predicted a heavy snowfall, but we were not actually prepared for it. Perhaps the mild winters of the past several years have lulled us to sleep, but we were in for a rude awakening. In any event, it made us aware of how helpless we are when faced with the wilder side of nature.

We may get the idea that our civilization is so advanced, and our technology is refined to the place that we are invincible. It only takes a winter storm of major proportions to reduce our thinking to the basics of eating, sleeping, and keeping warm.

It seems that the more modern the convenience, the greater was the inconvenience during this time. What good was a heat pump with no electricity to power it? The microwave oven sat useless, the humming of the furnace was silenced and our water supply was cut off with no power to run the water pump. We were more fortunate than some of the others who had all-electric homes, as we had natural gas and could continue to cook as usual. Our power was off for four and half days but some of our neighbors are still without electricity.

While we suffered only mild inconveniences, others faced actual hardship and danger. We read of those on ventilators and oxygen, stranded up rural roads with snow piling up relentlessly and it makes us doubly thankful that we were warm, healthy and safe.

People who live out in the country are better equipped to face this type of emergency, since many homes use wood heat routinely. Also, kerosene heaters are standard equipment and Coleman lanterns and camping stoves are stored for summertime use. Almost every country home has a kerosene lamp and a supply of candles. We could have managed for a much longer period of time if it had been necessary.

With a cellar full of canned food and a deep freezer full of meat and vegetables, we would not have gone hungry. We buried the food from the refrigerator in a snow bank, but the deep freezer was a worry. It stayed frozen solid, but in a few more days it would have begun to thaw.

How did we manage in the old days without all these conveniences? It was much easier, with the pitcher pump that was man (or boy) powered and our water supply was not dependent upon electricity. The outdoor johnny house never needed flushing and was faithful, winter and summer. All our food was canned, dried, cured, or pickled, and there was no danger of spoilage by thawing.

A trip to the grocery store was not a necessity, as the milk cow provided milk, butter, and cottage cheese and the flock of laying hens supplied all the eggs we needed. Before our house was wired for electricity, we had gaslights, a gas Servel refrigerator and a Maytag wringer washer powered by a gasoline motor. A snowstorm such as the one we have just come through would not have altered our way of life one bit.

The snowstorm was a blessing, in many ways. Homes were opened to neighbors, who were without heat, and old fashioned kindness and hospitality prevailed. Families were brought closer together as the hectic pace of life came to a virtual standstill and people had to rely on each other for conversation and fellowship. With the TV screens silent, and computer games impossible, the old-timey board games were dusted off and put to use. Card games were played by the light of kerosene lamps and the flickering flame of candles. Even the little ones enjoyed the coziness and cheer, as we ate fresh-baked cookies and buttery popcorn.

Mountain people have always been known for their resourcefulness and ability to cope under adverse conditions. I am sure that many stories will surface about this storm, stories of heroism, pure grit and fortitude. Stories will be told of frightening experiences of the big snowstorm of January, 1994. But there will be heart-warming memories as well, of how neighbors banded together to ride out the storm. It was a week dropped out of time, when we were able to get a little taste of "how things used to be."

I will have to confess that when our household saw the power company truck plow its way up the hill,

followed by the tree-cutting outfit, we
gave a loud cheer. It was good to
return to the present.

The Charleston Gazette
January 14, 1994

The Clay County Free Press
January 19, 1994

CHAPTER 2

HOLIDAYS AND HAPPY DAYS

"And I do come home at Christmas.
We all do, or we all should.
We all come home, or ought
to come home, for a short holiday—
the longer, the better—"

...Charles Dickens

Home for Christmas—the very thought revives old memories, emotions and longings. In our minds, we relive the past with friends and loved ones, some of them now gone, in sweet recollection. Memories are a gift of God that is not destroyed by death.

My earliest memories of Christmas are compounded of the tantalizing smell of warm candle wax, combined with the tangy fragrance of pine needles. We had no electricity and the pine tree (always a short-needled hemlock) was studded with tiny brass candleholders that clipped on the limbs. In the holders were placed small, twisted Christmas candles that were lit on Christmas Eve.

I can't remember much about the presents but I do remember cuddling up close to Mom while she recited to us the old Christmas story. I can see the firelight twinkling, casting shadows in the corners and lighting up Mom's face. I still think it is the greatest story ever told—of God's immeasurable love to man, in sending down His most perfect gift—Jesus.

I could feel myself on a lonely hillside with the shepherds, watching the sheep under a star-studded sky. The fire in the gas stove would turn to a flickering campfire in my imagination, and I would draw my shepherd's robe tighter around me and listen to the low murmur of conversation among the other shepherds. Mom's voice would quicken with excitement as she described the sudden appearance of the angel bringing "good tidings of great joy." I could see the glory of the Lord shining about me and the shiver of fear that ran through my body was real.

In my mind's eye, the room was populated with a host of angels singing, "Glory to God in the highest, and on earth peace, good will toward man."

Then as she described the hasty trip to Bethlehem, made by the shepherds to see for themselves this marvelous thing that had come to pass, I felt myself running along after them. My shepherd's cloak flapped around my short legs as I scurried to keep up with the excited shepherds. Breathless and tired, we would reach the stable.

As Mom's voice went on and on, I would enter the stable with the shepherds. The stable would have a warm, inviting smell just like our old barn, the dry, sweet odor of hay and the homey, warm smell of the animals. Awed, I would tiptoe to the manger where the tiny baby lay. Mary would be there, tired yet radiant. We were familiar with the sweetness of newborn babies, yet this was a special baby—and lying on the hay in a manger!

We invariably interrupted Mom at this point in the story, highly incensed because there was no room for

Jesus in the inn. "We would have made room for Him, Mommy," we would say indignantly. "Mary could have had my bed!" (No room, no time for Jesus, is the cry of men today.)

To many people, the story ends there. Jesus, the baby, is something that they take out, just as a tree ornament, to dust off and display for a few days during this season of the year. Then after Christmas, He is put back on the shelf with the other decorations and forgotten about until next year.

I am so glad that the story did not end with the birth of Jesus. The story of the Nativity is a beautiful one and I love it. But the life, death, and resurrection of the man Jesus means everything to us today. He brought the plan of salvation that is our only hope. Of course, when I was a child, I was not aware of all of this. I rejoiced in the story of Baby Jesus, which through the years has not lost any of its charm. It is the background of my Christmas memories, woven with the threads of family love and tied with the precious remembrances of happy times together. Christmas is a time to show love unashamedly, to tie the family ties a little tighter, and to express appreciation to each member. It is a time to get together, to pile high the groaning board, to rejoice in the security of family love.

Most of all, it is a time to reflect on the greatest gift the world has ever known and what it means to each of us individually. Yes, Jesus is more than a baby born in a manger. St. John 1:14 says, "And the Word was made flesh, and dwelt among us (and we beheld His glory, the glory as of the only begotten of the Father) full of grace and truth." What does this mean to us?

He was the supreme sacrifice for our sins, and the only way to be saved and redeemed back into fellowship with the Father. "He was wounded for our transgressions, He was bruised for our iniquities; the chastisement of our peace was upon Him, and with His stripes we are healed." Isaiah 53:5

No wonder that the angel carried good tidings of great joy. I pray that the presence of Jesus in each of your hearts will bring great joy. May God's love be with you as we celebrate the birth of His Son.

The Clay County Free Press
December 26, 1984

More than 50 years (60, now) a little girl with skinny blonde pigtails is waiting for Christmas. It seemed the day would never end but night is finally deepening around the little house perched on the bank of Summer's Fork Creek.

Summer's Fork flows into Little Laurel Creek, which runs into Big Laurel Creek, which in turn empties into Elk River, which turns its waters into the Kanawha River, which sweeps into the Ohio River, which rolls into the mighty Mississippi, which slides smoothly into the sea.

The little girl knew nothing of this, of course. Her whole world consisted of the little house, with its Wallrite-papered walls and tar paper roof which housed her, her mother and father and a younger brother and baby sister. Too, there were her grandpa and grandma, who lived across the yard in their own bigger house, with a porch on the front, a porch on the back, and a porch on the side. Their house boasted a tar paper roof also, with rough outside boards silvered by the rain and snow of many winters. Woodbine and rambler roses crept up the front porch posts and shaded the old porch swing in the summer, and made a snug hideaway for little girls.

Grandpa, with his pipe always clenched in his toothless gums and Grandma, with her gold-framed spectacles perched on the end of her nose, were extra special people to the little girl. As a matter of fact, it was her grandmother, with her healing hands, who had brought both her and her little sister into the world. For some reason, she hadn't delivered her brother, but instead old Doc Smith had brought him in his mysterious black bag.

But right now, she wasn't thinking about them, or anyone else, for that matter. Her whole being was concentrated fiercely on making the day pass as soon as possible and speeding up the night. For this was THE NIGHT!

It had taken days and days to arrive to this point. It seemed that she had waited forever for the night to finally come, although she had enjoyed each prior day with feverish excitement. She thought about the cold, snowy day that her father pulled the homemade wooden sled up the hill to the woods and came back with the Hemlock pine tree, covered with its short, green needles. It had to be adjusted just right and her father had even drilled a few holes down one side of the trunk to insert extra branches to balance the beauty of the tree.

It had been trimmed so carefully with fragile glass balls, metallic icicles and bright-colored, twisted candles inserted into tiny brass candleholders that clipped tightly to the tree limbs. It had stood there for days, with its precious candles and tonight they were going to light them!

Her mother had spent lots of hours in the kitchen, baking pies and cookies, and gingerbread men. She had let the little girl sprinkle red and green colored sugar on the cookies that were shaped like stars and angels and Christmas trees. The tiny baby sister was too young to know anything that was going on, and her younger brother was mostly a pest. Oh, she loved him dearly, and guarded him with maternal devotion, but sometimes he was a trial.

She is watching out the window with rapt attention at the clear winter sky. The stars blink and twinkle and seem to reflect the bubbling excitement that threatens to spill out of her at any time. Her brother, pulling a paper box with a shoe string and making "choo-choo" noises, bumps into the back of her legs and earns himself a dirty look. Soon, however, she has her arm around his neck and is telling him of the gifts they are sure to find under the tree the next morning. His eyes sparkle in anticipation, and soon both of them are jumping in delight.

It is growing dark now and their mother comes in to light the gas mantles. Her chores over for the day, she sits down in the rocking chair to read the Bible to the children. The little girl leans on the arm of her mother's chair while her brother plays quietly at her feet. Many of the words are over her head, but she listens, enchanted, as her mother reads the beloved story.

Her attention is caught by the words, "And she brought forth her firstborn Son, and wrapped Him in swaddling clothes and laid Him in a manger, because there was no room for them in the inn."

She thought of Grandpa's old log barn and pictured the rough manger where the cows munched their hay. She could see the tiny newborn baby bedded down in a mound of sweet-smelling hay and she wished she could pick him up and hold him. She grew sleepy as her mother's voice read on and on, and barely made it through her "Now I lay me down to sleep" prayer.

Almost in a daze, she watches her father light the candles on the tree. From candle to candle he moves the wooden match, as each twisted candle flares and lights. Her mother turns out the gas mantle and now there is only the glow from the candle-lit tree to illuminate the room. The gas fire reflects the candle glow and the room is rich in love and contentment.

The little girl drifts off to sleep, floating on the aroma of candle wax and warm pine needles. Her last conscious thought is of a helpless, newborn baby, looking much like her own baby sister, reaching out to her from the manger in Grandpa's barn.

In the morning, she is awakened by her father, who is pulling the covers from her and gently shaking her shoulder. Grinning widely, he says, "Get up and see what is under the tree for you!" Suddenly wide-awake, she jumps out of bed and runs to the tree.

She doesn't see the tricycle sitting there for her brother, or any of the other presents. Her attention is focused on the doll that is reaching out for her. A warm rush of maternal love flows through her as she cuddles the doll, with its composition head and cloth body, close to her. It is her own, her very own baby.

Many Christmases have come and gone and the little girl is now a mother and a grandmother (and a great-grandmother) many times over. But she has never forgotten that special Christmas so long ago, when she became a mother.

The Clay Herald
December 19, 1988

The Charleston Gazette
December 20, 1991

A pale November sun shines weakly through the rifted clouds and turns a broomsage patch on the hill to dull gold. A handful of brown leaves, the only ones remaining, flutter in the brisk air from the top of the chestnut tree. The weeping willow tree, that waved bright green pennants in the air all summer long, now stands forlorn and naked. Across the creek the sycamores stand with their bone white arms stretched skyward. Not a cricket chirps, not a flower blooms. November is quietly putting the land to sleep for its long winter's nap, to awake refreshed once more in the spring.

November is redeemed by Thanksgiving, that heart-warming holiday that tightens the family ties a little tighter and makes the hearth fires burn a little brighter. Memories of Thanksgivings past flood the mind, bright memories of long-ago days when life was more simple and the days much longer. It seemed that we had to wait forever for a holiday to finally arrive. The eager anticipation was almost as good as the reality as we waited and planned.

Thanksgiving was always a family get-together, with a multitude of aunts, uncles, cousins, grandpas and grandmas. I can still see Grandpa O'Dell at his accustomed place at the table, his head bowed low as the blessing was asked. Grandpa never learned to wear his store-bought teeth but it didn't seem to hinder his eating at all. He was a short man, his back arrow straight even after he grew old, and he loved company. Anyone visiting at mealtime was forced to join the family around the table and he also loved to visit other homes for food and fellowship.

We watched anxiously as Mom began planning the holiday meal a day or so in advance. When I was little, we never had turkey as we do now, but there were always two or three fat roasting hens waiting to be stuffed and placed in the oven. Down through the years, I can still smell the mouth-watering aroma of the onion, celery and sage dressing. The skin on the chickens would turn brown and crispy and the dressing would be literally bursting through the tender goodness.

Mom always baked a variety of pies, from the creamy, brown butterscotch ones to apple and pumpkin. Nothing smells more like Thanksgiving than the spicy fragrance of a pumpkin pie taken hot from the oven.

Salad was Daddy's specialty. He would create original ones—I still remember the grape and cheese concoction he made one year. It was different. There would be mashed potatoes swimming in giblet gravy, sweet potatoes bathed in butter and brown sugar, green beans simmered with bacon, fresh cranberry sauce, fluffy hot rolls and our own real cow butter. Mom nearly always made the orange-coconut cake that was reserved for special occasions.

The memories glow brighter of bygone days, where loved ones now gone once more live and love, and never grow old. We are making memories now for our own children and grandchildren. All too soon, the good times that we are now enjoying will be part of the past. Let us make precious memories that can be taken down, dusted, and relived once more by those who are walking in our footsteps.

Thanksgiving makes us more aware of our multitude of blessings, although I am deeply grateful for every day that the Lord lets me live. It is impossible to thank God for all the blessings He does bestow and it makes a person feel so humble when we begin counting them, one by one. I am thankful for the little home I grew up in—a plain Jenny Lind house of unpainted boards and sprawling rooms. Yet, it was full of love and security and the things that money cannot buy. We, as children, were content with a mother and father who loved one another, and in turn loved and wanted each of us.

Above all, we were taught from the very beginning of a Father's love and concern for us and of our obligations to Him. Our parent's example of a real faith in God inspired us more than a thousand sermons. I am deeply grateful for my own home, for my children and grandchildren.

My heart is full of thankfulness this Thanksgiving season—and it is still for the things that money can't buy. A home full of love and contentment, peace between my soul and God, our grandchildren like "olive plants round about our table"—these are the real treasures of life.

Above all, let us never forget where our blessings come from. Psalms

100:4 tells us, "Enter into His gates with thanksgiving and into His courts with praise: be thankful unto Him, and bless His name."

The Clay County Free Press
November 23, 1983

Echoes of yesterday . . . years that run together . . . break into bright blossoms of memory . . .then blend into the smooth-flowing river of the past.

The sagey smell of my turkey roasting wafts through the kitchen and I am transported to that old house again. . . the oldest of seven kids filling the house to the brim . . . underfoot, fussing some among ourselves, eagerly awaiting the festive meal . . . the homey smell of onion-sage dressing makes our mouths water and we can hardly wait until the chickens are roasted to a turn and brought to the table, brown and tender . . . the rows of butterscotch, coconut and cherry pies lined up on the shelves in the "junk room" . . . where Mom kept her jars of home canned food stored behind a curtain . . . Daddy concentrating deeply as he built one of his special salads . . .

Other memories . . . sharp, cutting edges that twist and hurt . . .a nursing home and Daddy . . . face

twisted with pain and paralysis . . .
being fed turkey and dressing on
Thanksgiving Day . . . restaurants
closed and our holiday dinner purchased
from a 7-Eleven store . . . choked down
through our tears . . .

The turkey is done and I begin
putting our favorite dishes on the
table . . . buttered broccoli and
cauliflower, cranberry-pineapple salad,
fresh fruit salad, pumpkin pie and
carrot cake . . . my mind goes back . .

Mom, tired but triumphant . . face
flushed with heat from the oven . . .
proudly bearing pans of yeasty,
homemade rolls, brown and crusty, to
the table . . . the cranberry sauce
made from fresh cranberries, tart and
tangy . . . eleven heads, including
Grandpa, bowed over the meal . . . the
oil-cloth covered table . . . the
young'ens crammed tight together on the
homemade wooden bench behind the table
. . . Daddy intoning a heartfelt thanks
as he asked God's blessings on the food
and on us . . . the taste of food on my
tongue . . .

But it wasn't just the food that I
remember . . . but that warm, secure
feeling of "home" . . . we knew we were
loved and wanted . . in that old,
leaky, drafty, Jenny Lind house that
never saw a drop of paint . . . it was
full of love and tenderness . . . and
we were taught of God's great love that
envelopes and guides us . . .

That love was the last thing I felt from Daddy . . . after his last words were spoken to me . . . telling me that he loved me . . . I never heard him speak again . . . after speech was gone, his eyes, full of love, followed us around the room . . . the stroke had affected his mind, and ravaged his body . . . yet love was tangible . . . it was the last thing I felt from him . . . love . .

The grandchildren, as rowdy and noisy as we used to be, crowd around the table on the back porch . . . famished, and eager for food . . . energetic little boys and girls with healthy minds and healthy bodies . . . do they feel this love of family as we did? Do they feel secure in the knowledge that they are truly loved and wanted . . . and cherished? I hope that memories of home and family will always be a bright beacon in their minds . . . a beacon to lead them home again . . . no matter how far afield they roam . . . to family love and unity . . .

Thanksgiving Day draws to a close . . . the pink sunset has slipped behind the hills and night is darkening the skies . . . tiny, twinkling stars glitter upon a frost-covered landscape . . . it has been a good day with the children and grandchildren . . . a day to commit to memory and relive in some future time . . . a day rich in love and warm companionship . . .

Thank God for the real blessings .
. . the love of God for us . . . the
love for family and home . . . the love
for one another . . . these are the
things that last . . .

The Charleston Gazette
November 27, 1992

Mountain folk have always been a
superstitious bunch. I was brought up
on premonitions and tokens (I never saw
one, but I was scared to death that I
would).

As children, we loved to gather
around Mom and listen to her recite the
old ghost tales that had been handed
down by her mother—and more than
likely, had been told for generations.
We would be deliciously frightened out
of our wits and afraid to go to bed at
night. We loved it.

There was the tale about the
family who moved here from Pennsylvania
many years ago to a lonely knoll near
Twistabout Ridge. It seemed that the
mother of the family was expecting a
baby, and a young hired girl came with
them, who was also pregnant. The mother
was sickly, so they hired another girl
to come in and help with the work.

It was told that there were three
babies born in that little house, all
fathered by the same man. About that
time, the wife died a mysterious death

51

and the word "poison" was whispered about in the neighborhood. It was also told that they couldn't keep her tongue in her mouth after she died.

Strange things began happening; people began to see and hear things that could not be explained. After his wife died, the man married the last girl who had come to help with the housework. She was soon expecting again and had one little dead baby after another. They were buried on another lonely ridge near there, where the pine trees sighed and moaned in the night winds.

One day the father was sitting at the table, when he suddenly jumped up and began leaping in the air and grabbing at invisible objects. "Oh, I see her," he cried, "She's coming down and she has a bunch of little babies around her!"

I can still hear my Aunt Addie's voice (she was a spellbinding storyteller) as she said, "Maw told me these things, and I know she wouldn't lie."

Her Aunt Harriet stayed all night once in the house after the father had died and when she came home, she vowed that she would never stay there again. When Maw questioned her, she said, "After I went to bed last night, a little, low woman with long black hair, all dressed in white, came and stood by my bed. And Alice, her tongue was hanging out."

One time there was to be a burial in that same cemetery (another little baby) and Liberty Grade School down on Twistabout was dismissed for the afternoon in order for the school children to attend.

My mother was in this group of children and she said that when they got near the cemetery, a terrible fear came over the whole group and they turned with one accord and began running and screaming back toward the school.

To this day, she cannot explain just what happened. Her father, Grandpa Huge, was a very levelheaded, calm man but he made the statement that it was one cemetery that he wouldn't want to mess around, even in broad daylight.

One of the neighbors was picking blackberries along the road on that same property and he looked up and saw a little, short woman, wearing a straw hat, walking up the road toward him. He continued picking berries, intending to speak to her when she got close. When she came near him, she just disappeared. He said he never knew what happened to her.

Right below this farm was an old log cabin that was supposed to be haunted. People who lived in this cabin told of unexplained happenings. It was rumored that a "bad" woman once lived there and had been stoned to death and her body left under the pile of stones.

It seemed that the cabin had a front door that no one could keep closed—in the middle of the night it would open of its own accord.

Sometimes they would hear "something" come screaming down the hill from the cemetery and circle the house. Later they would find tracks that looked like the print of a lady's small, high-heeled shoe.

Then they would hear what sounded like a horse running with a loose shoe. It would run 'round and 'round the house, then across the bridge, its loose shoe clattering on the boards. But they never saw anything.

The tale that I liked most to hear was the "Ha'nted Mud Hole." Actually, it was probably the huge oak tree above the mudhole that was "ha'nted," as it was reputed that someone was once hanged from that very tree.

My grandmother was coming past there one time, with two of her sons who were just little tots, when a dog appeared beside them. He was running along, about a foot above the road, and his feet never touched the ground. One of the boys yelled, "Maw, Maw, did you see that flying dog?"

Many of the neighbors on Twistabout Ridge would hear a huge object, like a crosstie, come hurtling down from the top of the old oak tree and plunge to the ground—although they never saw a thing. Not a leaf or twig would stir, yet it could be heard plainly.

There were many, many other unexplained happenings there but, after the tree was cut down, the haunting ended.

I am not saying that these tales are true; I am telling them to you just as they were told to me—many times in the dark of night, when black clouds cast shadows over the moon and the air was filled with mysterious rustlings. They were believable then.

The Charleston Gazette
October 28, 1994

The Clay County Free Press
November 2, 1994

A thin sickle moon reclines on his back and tries to entice the evening star into the cradle of his arms. A warm and balmy southerly wind is blowing, reminding me of one of Mom's old sayings, "When the south wind blows, the ghosts rise up from the graveyard."

Several years ago when my brother Ronnie was a half-grown lad, he had a hair-raising experience about this time of year. It was just before Hallowe'en and he had gone home with his friend Kermit to watch "Chiller" on television. The hour was late and the program had been especially scary that night. Ronnie was more than a little apprehensive about journeying home all alone but he bravely struck out.

Now Kermit lived at the top of a mountain and to reach home, Ronnie had to pass the church and the adjoining cemetery. He didn't have a flashlight but the moon was shining and full. That is, when thin, wispy clouds didn't float across the face of it, making the night even blacker and creating eerie shadows across his path.

There was mysterious rustling in the underbrush above the road and the sudden blood-curdling quaver of a screech owl momentarily turned him to stone. Blood drained to his feet, and his heart pounded madly. He walked faster around the curve in the road while the trees seemed to reach out bony, menacing arms to grab him.

Just as he glimpsed the first pale tombstones shimmering in the moonlight, he thought he heard softly padded footsteps behind him. He stopped and there was no sound. Hurriedly, he half-ran for a few more paces and this time he was sure that someone was following him. His mouth dry, he halted again and listened. There was no movement, no noise. In blind panic, he began running. This time there was no mistaking the furtive footsteps behind him.

Ice froze in his veins and he looked back once again. On one side of the road, the cemetery fence shone white and orderly rows of tombstones reflected the moonlight. Right then, in the road, he could barely make out the shape of a dark object that moved slightly.

Terror-stricken, he dropped to his knees and his groping fingers found a rock slightly larger than his fist. With courage born of desperation, he flung the missile and ran for his life. There was an unearthly howl from the creature but he didn't wait to investigate. His speed never abated until he reached the sanctuary of his home, which had never been so welcome. He crept into his bed with a sigh of relief and never uncovered his head until morning.

The next day he walked out into the yard to be greeted by Freckles, his faithful dog, who had a curiously swollen head. Loyal Freckles, who had waited patiently outside Kermit's home to follow his master and guard him from all danger.

My sister Jeannie had her most terrifying experience when she was a teenager. The little house that Mom and Daddy lived in when they were first married and was used from time to time by some of us, was vacant at the moment. The electricity was still turned on in it and we used it to store various items. Mom sent Jeannie one

dark night to get something that she
needed from it and she couldn't find a
flashlight. With faint heart and
trembling legs, Jeannie set out anyway,
relying on her sense of direction to
lead her through the darkness.

The night was black as pitch, with
that palatable blackness that seems to
breathe danger. She crept across the
yard, then timidly tiptoed across the
footbridge that spanned a deep ditch.
The night was curiously quiet; only the
sounds of her thudding heart and
faltering footsteps could be heard. The
journey down the path seemed endless
and as she passed the Lombardy poplar
tree, she looked back at the tiny
square of light shining through the
kitchen window, reflecting home and
safety.

It seemed forever before she
reached the front porch of the old
house and felt her way to the front
door. It screeched as she slowly opened
it, sending her already racing heart
into fresh panic and weakening her
knees. Cautiously, she slid her hand
around the door facing, and fumbled for
the light switch. Her hand suddenly
closed over another hand on the wall.
With a shriek of pure terror, she held
on for dear life. She was afraid to let
go, and afraid to hold on. In her
agitation, her wrist caught on the
light switch and flipped it on. As
light flooded the room, she realized
that she was holding one of her hands

tight in the grip of the other. These days you can't trust anybody.

It used to be such fun, when we were kids, to huddle in the corner of a room with the lights off and tell delicious ghost stories designed to scare the pants off us. A real fear however, when you were a child, is a different thing. Andy went through a period of time (months, it seemed) when he dreamed terror-stricken dreams of bears every night. It got so bad that he was afraid to go to sleep because he knew he would have dreams about bears.

Matthew was afraid of the dark. He was sure that terrible monsters and wicked beings lurked in the blackness, ready to grab him and carry him away. I can remember that he would send Crystal (and she two years younger) ahead of him up the stairs to turn on the lights at bedtime.

I didn't know until years later, when they were both married and away from home, that she charged him a quarter for each time she did it for him. No wonder the poor kid never had any allowance left for himself.

The Clay County Free Press
October 31, 1984

The Charleston Gazette
October 30, 1992

A thin spiral of smoke from a neighboring chimney prompts a quick dash to the calendar to verify that it is indeed summer and the Fourth of July is just around the corner. This cool spell reminds me of the one we had one summer while Crystal was still home. She slept late one morning and bleary-eyed, opened the door to be greeted by a blast of 40° weather. "What did I do?" she asked in bewilderment, "Sleep through summer?"

I am duck sitting this week and it has been quite an experience. I made the mistake of hatching out one lone duck egg (for grandson Aaron) in an incubator with some banty eggs. I felt a maternal bond as I saw him kick his way out of a large green egg and obviously he must have felt the same bonding process.

He must be a Mallard and white duck mix, with yellow wing tips and a yellow chest on a black body. He also has a tiny yellow streak at the corner of each eye, giving him a jaunty, devil-may-care look. He also wants someone near him all the time.

I installed him in a laundry basket in the kitchen, but the minute I step out of sight, he sets up a frantic, loud peeping. As any mother knows, you can't spend every moment with your child. So I set a small radio against the laundry basket and turned it to a country and western station. He sticks his beak through a hole in the basket and goes to sleep with guitar music twanging in his ear.

Aaron calls him "Darkwing" (naturally) and he is an inseparable companion to the boys. He swims in the pool with them, skimming and diving. They have to be careful about stepping on him, as he tags so closely to their heels that one misstep would be disastrous. When we go down to the creek each day, he's not about to get in that water alone.

I throw him out; he flaps through the water and climbs the bank to huddle on my feet reproachfully. I am sure that if I got out in the water and paddled with him, he would be content. I can't figure out if he thinks I am a duck, or he is a people. The next time Patty leaves for a week, I think I will keep the boys and let her take the duck.

He's doing fine, though, although I think he has an achybreaky heart. And I have developed honky-tonk ears.

We have some baby banties, not much bigger than a cotton ball, following their mothers and scratching contentedly. The silver-laced Wyandotte pullets are well on their way to henhood and brown country eggs. There are two Rhode Island Red roosters (or Redeyed Rolands, as someone asked for in the Farm Store) who are beginning to spar and challenge one another. I have trouble getting rid of the chickens I don't want, as I can't bear to kill them.

Mom asked my nephew Freddie to catch one of her hens and she would cook him a pot of chicken and dumplings. He looked at her like she was Lizzie Borden and exclaimed in horror, "You don't think that I would eat something that I have been feeding, do you?"

The Fourth of July meant home—fried chicken to us, along with fresh half-runner green beans and lemonade. (I would hide in the house while Mom chopped off the chickens' heads.) It meant picnicking and swimming down on Big Laurel Creek, with a cold watermelon to end the day. I can still feel that cool dampness that emanated from the very creek itself and see the rhododendron and hemlock that bordered its banks. White water honeysuckle bloomed in the edge of the water, its sweet scent perfuming the air. Of all the fragrances that nature produces, the scent of water honeysuckle is most haunting to me. I have read that smells will trigger almost-forgotten memories quicker than any of our other senses and I believe it.

Just the memory of that scent brings back the carefree days of childhood, wading in the creek and building sandcastles. It's funny how you forget the bad things like stone bruises (Daddy opened them with a razor blade—now tell me why you never hear of them anymore) the itchy poison ivy and stubbed toes, and remember mostly the good things.

To us, the Fourth of July meant the freedom to go where we wished, to run and play as hard as we could, and to stuff ourselves with good country food. It meant firecrackers and watermelon and coming home dead-tired. To my grandchildren, it means virtually the same thing. They don't realize that it also means memories for the future.

Big Laurel Creek is now a public fishing area, and the quiet solitude is gone. No doubt the water honeysuckles are gone too, but the good memories still linger.

The Charleston Gazette
July 3, 1992

Father's Day—a special day for remembering and I am remembering the things that Daddy taught us.

He taught us a love and an appreciation for nature that many people take for granted. He would point out the fragrant glory of an apple tree in bloom and show us the intricate perfection of a tiny violet cupped in one palm. He couldn't walk through the fields without picking a bouquet of wild flowers for Mom, or for one of us.

He loved spring and in the dead of winter would describe its coming in such graphic detail that we could feel the soft, new grass under our bare feet, hear the trill of the songbirds as they built their nests and smell the wild plum blossoms in the air.

After a summer shower, when a rainbow arched high over Pilot Knob, he would call our attention to how the colors blended one into another. The glory of a sunset, streaked with amethyst, crimson and gold, thrilled him beyond words—and he enjoyed it so much more when he could share it with us.

We learned early the pleasures of the outdoors—camping out along a trout stream, eating our breakfast from a tin pan as the swift water rippled and sparkled in the sun and the smell of pine trees was strong in the air. We learned about the woods in the fall, when we camped out again at Hickory Knob during squirrel season. There was a quiet glow about Daddy as he showed us an especially showy maple tree decked out in its fall colors. He wanted us to love nature as he did—and we do.

I can remember how he pulled us on a sled after a snowfall and how he would catch snowflakes on his glove to show us that no two were ever alike. He had a zest for living that spilled over and caught in us.

Daddy taught us to work and to take pride in doing a job well. How many times we heard the old adage, "A job worth doing is worth doing well," and "Do it right the first time, then you won't have to lick your calf over." We would hear this as he made us go over the row of corn that we had half-hoed until we did it to suit him. This was a valuable lesson, and one that helps me to this day.

He taught us to value our time, and not waste it on unhappy pursuits. Sometimes Larry and I would spend a morning bickering and fighting. Daddy would tell us, and the words are still so clear today, that we had wasted that much of our life. "You can never go back and live that time over," he would tell us solemnly, "You could have been happy and having fun, and you wasted it in fussing."

He taught us a reverence for older people, to respect their age and the wisdom that many years had brought them. I have many rewarding friendships with older people that I may have missed otherwise.

Daddy gave out affection unrestrainedly and we learned to do the same. He loved Mom and us and everyone around him. I have seen him put his arm around Mom in church, or take her hand when we were walking and the glow of love encircled us. He loved babies—anybody's babies—and this heritage has been passed down to my own children. My six-foot sons will pick up and cuddle a baby in public without embarrassment.

The most important thing that Daddy taught us was God's love for us. He taught us, by word and pure example, the worth of our own souls. We learned early the way of salvation and letting God lead and direct our lives. Daddy taught us to pray and I have never heard anyone pray like he did. He had a secret place of prayer, down in the woods beside a big rock. And it was no secret when he prayed. Even if we couldn't have heard him (which we did and Daddy's prayers still ring in my ears) we could tell by his glowing face that he had been talking to God. He brought us up in the way that we should go and if some of us have departed from it, I am sure that they have not forgotten.

Daddy taught us things that no one else could have. A special day for remembering? I remember Daddy every day of my life.

The Clay County Free Press
June 16, 1982

The Charleston Gazette
June 19, 1992

Memorial Day and memories . . . We used to call it Decoration Day and we decorated the family graves with flowers.

A solitary songbird breaks forth in a salute to the day, though the skies are yet dark and dawn has not arrived. It is a fitting symbol for the beginning of this Memorial Day weekend. All day yesterday, this holiday weighed on my mind—Memorial Days past and gone, but not forgotten.

The rhododendron is beginning to bloom now; it seems that it was always blooming when we were kids walking down the woodsy path to the family cemetery. We cousins skipped along happily, gathering the white clusters of rhododendron bloom, daisies and wild roses. Our hearts were light, as death had little meaning then. Our mothers took bouquets of fragrant peonies, rambler roses and sweet-smelling irises. We covered the graves of Grandma Alice, Grandpa Huge and then ran off to play. Some of our cousins now are gone. Goodbye, Ann . . .

The cemetery beside our church was familiar and loved. I always put wild roses on Grandma O'Dell's grave, for she loved them. Daddy planted a bleeding heart there for the same reason. Yet, the wild, sweet ferns of early spring always brings back memories of Grandma. I was only seven when she died, yet I remember gathering ferns with her when we were on a camping trip. Memories of Grandpa are more piercing and I miss him still . .

. Now there are more . . . Daddy, a grandbaby, a nephew . . . Goodbye David . . . Goodbye, Jennifer Alyce . . .

As I drove past Hickory Knob late yesterday evening, past the blooming little laurel and rhododendron thickets, I thought of the handsome boy who was killed in Korea and lies buried high on a lonesome ridge there in the hills. How he loved the hills! He was so anxious to come home, but he was killed on Memorial Day, May 30. Now he is forever home . . . Goodbye, Myles . . .

Mom says that the longer you live, the more people you have to be concerned about and I am sure this is true. We also lose them, miss them and mourn them. Yet, there are more people to love . . . as our family grows by leaps and bounds, the love grows also . . . As God magnifies the love, He provides the comfort needed when the time comes for mourning . . .

Memorial Day brings memories to all of us . . . Some grievous and heart-wrenching . . . Some sad and bittersweet . . . Some comforting . . . But we remember . . .

The Clay Herald
May 28, 1990

As far back as I can remember, my mother's hands were always busy. Like the dipper in the water bucket, or the

button on the toilet door, it was taken
for granted that she would always be
there when we needed her. All the years
when I was growing up, I thought she
ate the chicken neck because she liked
it the best. It is only in becoming a
mother that one can understand the
heart of a mother.

Early in the morning, I awakened
to the sound of her hands at work in
the kitchen. Long before daylight, she
was up preparing breakfast for Daddy
and her brood of hungry children. I
could hear the soft slap of her hands
kneading the biscuit dough, the muffled
thud as she closed the oven door and
the scrape of the biscuit cutter as she
cleaned the flour from the metal
cabinet top she used for a dough board.

Soon the bubbling sound of the
percolator was heard as the smell of
freshly brewed coffee filled the house,
mixed with the tantalizing, smoky aroma
of frying bacon. I would snuggle back
in my warm covers, content in the
knowledge that I could sleep awhile
longer. Yet today, the sound of someone
preparing breakfast while I am still in
bed brings back that secure childhood
feeling.

When I awoke again, it was to her
hands pulling back the covers and
telling us to "get up—breakfast is
ready." After we soused our faces in
the tin wash-pan, we sat down to a real
country breakfast—mounds of hot,
fluffy biscuits, bacon and eggs,

sometimes our own home-cured ham, homemade blackberry jelly, creamed tomatoes and fresh country butter. There was a hard day's work ahead for us on the farm and we ate heartily.

It is only in looking back that I realize how busy my mother was. Her hands were never still, but busy from daylight until dark and sometimes long after, moving swiftly from task to never-ending task. I can see her hands—gentle as they bathed the baby, vigorous as they attacked the weeds in the garden, swift as they meted out punishment to an unruly child. And our house was filled with children—Mom had all seven of us in 12 years.

It is strange how the years change one's perspective. When we moved to Davis Creek, Mom seemed ancient to me. She had four children then—I was seven and she was 27. Now she is 76 (84, in 1999) and it is amazing how young she was.

As I think back on those growing up years, I wonder how in the world she managed. Grandpa O'Dell moved in with us about that time and Cousin Leo was there part of the time.

Cooking for a family of 11 was in itself a monumental task. Mom had the biggest bread pan I have ever seen and sometimes she would bake an extra pie pan of biscuits. We had three hot meals a day, too. Her hands were ever busy above the stove, stirring huge cookers of food and turning over vast skillets of fried potatoes to brown.

We kept a milk cow and sometimes two, that had to be milked twice a day. Taking care of the milk was a time consuming job. She was quite particular about the milk, taking care to scald the utensils and strainer with boiling water after each use, her hands careful on the hot teakettle.

Churning had to be done almost every day, after the milk had been set out at room temperature to clabber. She would pour the clabbered milk into a five-gallon churn, scald the churn dash and lid and energetically pump the dash up and down in the churn. It was about the only time we saw Mom sit down. Even then, she would use the time to read the Bible while she churned.

After the butter was separated from the milk, I can see her hands grasp the dash firmly and with a quick, circular motion twirl it round and round until the butter was gathered in a lump on top of the milk. Then the butter had to be washed in successive changes of cold water until it ran clear, the buttermilk poured in jugs for our use and for a neighbor or two and the whole mess washed up and put away. She also did a lot of the milking until the boys got big enough to relieve her of the task.

Yes, her hands never seemed to stop. She made most of the clothing for us girls, and much of the boy's. At night she was forever mending blue jeans, the knees worn out from the eternal marble games. She braided our hair, tied up our sore toes and wiped our runny noses thousands of times.

I remember running to her one time with something I wanted done immediately. As she balanced a baby on one hip and stirred a pot of beans with the other hand, she exclaimed in exasperation "If I had seven heads and ten horns, I might be able to do that!" I imagine there were times that she wished for another pair of hands. Her hands could be quite tender when we needed consolation and I have also felt her palm applied heartily to my backside. Oh, that burning sting!

There came a time in my life when I went to her with a serious problem. I had agonized over telling her, putting it off until I no longer could. I waited for her explosive anger and instead, I felt her hands smoothing my hair. I will never forget her poor, overworked hands—hands that I had seen chapped and bleeding from hanging wet clothes on the clothesline in freezing, raw winter weather. Now those same hands were tenderly caressing my hair and comforting me. Those same hands had folded in prayer many times for me, held the Bible and taught me right from wrong. I could never repay her.

Her hands are beginning to look old now, the fingers knobby with arthritis and the veins blue and outstanding on the back. They are brown-speckled with old age spots and careworn. But they are the symbol of a mother's love and they are beautiful to me. And so is my mother.

The Clay Herald
May 6, 1991

The Charleston Gazette
August 22, 1991

My mother is shrinking. I don't know how long I have been looking down upon her, instead of looking up. We have a tendency to take our mothers for granted. They have been with us all of our lives and it seems that they will always be here.

She used to be bigger than life (Isn't it curious how your perspective changes as you grow older?). Her lap was big enough to cuddle and rock a baby, hold a bucket full of green beans while she strung and broke them or contain a mending basket of dungarees with worn-out knees. She always wore aprons, big enough to hold a picking of tomatoes from the garden, wipe the sweat from her brow when the sun got too hot or dry the tears from our eyes when we got hurt.

She seemed to grow in size when we misbehaved and had to be corrected. "Go

get a switch!" she would order. When
those dreaded words fell on our ears,
we knew she had reached her limit. I
wondered then why punishment was heaped
upon punishment in having to go after
our own weapons of execution. I realize
now that she was simply too busy to
take the time to get a switch.

If we made the mistake of bringing
in a flimsy, little switch, we were
promptly sent out again. It paid to get
an adequate one the first time. We were
treated to peach tree tea, birch tea
and sometimes those keen willow
branches. Those supple little limbs
would make you dance a jig. We were not
abused and contrary to modern thinking,
our psyches were not damaged nor our
personalities warped. On the contrary,
all seven of her children grew up into
responsible, caring adults, without a
criminal among us.

Now I wonder how she learned her
mothering skills so well. We have had
her for an example as a mother, a
grandmother and a great-grandmother.
However, her own mother died when she
was only 11 years old and her older
sisters married and started families of
their own. Who did she go to for advice
when a housekeeping problem loomed? We
all still call on Mom when expert
advice is needed. Each summer I find
myself asking her, "How long do you
process green beans?" or "Just how much
salt do you put in kraut?"

     In 82 years (84, in 1999), she has acquired much wisdom. Forced to abandon her schooling after the eighth grade, she read everything she could get in her hands. She is still an avid reader and has picked up a vast store of knowledge, as well as the practical knowledge of experience. All of her grandchildren call her "Mom-Granny," and they are as quick to call on her as her own children are. It seems that she knows a little something about any subject, from home remedies to poetry and we use her for an encyclopedia.

     Her garden has shrunk too, from the fields of corn and rows of green beans, to a dozen tomato plants and a short row of potatoes. She must have a few hills of cucumbers and some small rows of sweet corn, which she "wants to do by herself." She insists on mowing her own grass, but seems relieved when one of her sons comes by and does the task for her.

     Her cooking has also dwindled from the mountains of food that she heaped upon our homemade table to the small portions that she fixes for herself. It seems that our roles are becoming reversed, as I take her a tray of food and urge her to "eat a balanced diet." I see the grilled cheese sandwich and the cup of yogurt and remember with a pang the enormous bowls of food and huge platters of biscuits that once reposed there.

Her bosom was large and comforting and we poured out our childish hurts and teenage agonies upon her. I know that we have caused her many heartaches, secret tears and agonized prayers throughout the night. Yet, she never turned her back on any of us, or refused to lend a helping hand. Her family has expanded to include 26 grandchildren (three others are deceased) and more than 50 great-grandchildren. Although her stature has shrunk, her heart has expanded to include each newcomer. She eagerly awaits the birth of each new baby and still is an expert in newborn care.

She is so much a part of the fabric of our lives that it is impossible to imagine a life without her. She is vital, alert and active—feisty, even. We consider her indispensable.

Our mothers deserve honor on Mother's Day—and every day of their lives. My mother deserves much honor.

The Charleston Gazette
May 9, 1997

The Clay County Free Press
May 14, 1997

Easter came so quickly this year that it caught me quite unaware. It seemed that one-day it was winter and then it was Easter. It is not that the day has no meaning for me but that every day I rejoice in the risen Savior. When the Day Star arose in my heart, Christ's resurrection became a reality that I am thankful for every day of my life.

Still, I am glad that Easter, with its message of hope and life, comes with the return of spring upon the earth. All creation is praising God.

Easter was special when I was a youngster growing up at home. I can remember how we kids used to debate which was best—Easter, Christmas, or Father's Day. (Father's Day meant our annual family reunion where we spent the day frolicking and feasting with hordes of cousins and assorted kinfolk.)

Easter signaled the ending of winter and the advent of warm weather and freedom outdoors. We knew that it wouldn't be very long until we could shed the shackles of winter (mainly our shoes!) and revel in the tender grass of springtime. Daddy would tell us over and over again of the coming of spring—the cold, snowy days would pass, the warm sunshine would coax out the blooming flowers and budding leaves, the grass would grow and the tomatoes would get ripe. He always ended with the bit about the tomatoes. We would look at the world outside still locked in winter's grip and shiver in anticipation of the delights of coming spring.

To me, Easter meant frilly, new dresses made of permanent organdy or dotted swiss, handmade by Mom with lots of ruffles, lace and wide sashes tied in huge bows behind. After a steady diet of dresses made of gingham and feed sacks we felt like fairy princesses let out of our towers. We always had new white anklets and black patent leather shoes with a strap across the top. The boys got new western shirts and cowboy hats—that was Daddy's idea of sartorial elegance for the male gender.

Easter morning started early for us children and even earlier for Daddy. He would get out of a good warm bed at the crack of dawn to hide two or three dozen brightly-colored eggs in the yard before we woke up. Most of the time, it was cold and frosty and our fingers would freeze as we darted from a clump of grass to a nest of eggs hidden at the base of the rose bushes. It didn't dampen our enthusiasm though, as we shivered and searched for the very last egg.

Daddy would watch us and grin, throwing out broad hints to the smaller ones who weren't finding as many. I think now of what a sacrifice it was for Daddy to go out in the cold to provide us with that thrill of hunting eggs, although I am sure that he enjoyed it as much as we did.

I am thankful for a thoughtful father who provided us with many pleasures but I am more thankful that he showed by word and example a much deeper meaning to Easter and the Lord's resurrection.

Today is Good Friday; to much of the world it is simply a holiday. I think of what this Friday meant almost two thousand years ago—the darkest day the world has ever known. How desolate the disciples must have felt, those who had given up all to follow Jesus—when He was taken by cruel hands and hung on a cross! Oh, but the story did not end there—the good news is that Easter is not just colored eggs, new clothes, and baskets of goodies. But it is a risen Savior offering hope to the hopeless, strength to the weak and life to the dead—not only at this season, but every day. There is still time to find him. Jesus is still the answer.

The Clay Herald
April 4, 1988

CHAPTER THREE

KINFOLK AND HILLFOLK

"Long, long be my heart with such
memories fill'd!
Like the vase in which roses have once
been distill'd:
You may break, you may shatter the vase
if you will,
But the scent of the roses will hang
round it still."

...Thomas Moore

Grandpaw had a wonderful trunk. He brought it with him when he came to live with us; nobody knew how old it was then. As far back as I can remember it was there, ruling the bedroom.

It was an old, camel-back trunk; its domed top once covered with red velvet material and strips of embossed metal. The material had rotted and been torn away, but the metal shone bravely on. A wooden tray fit in the top of it, and when it was opened, it gave out a peculiar, metallic odor that belonged solely to Grandpaw's trunk

Of course we were never allowed in it and on the few occasions when we saw Grandpaw open it, we crowded around curiously. We were stopped with a stern, "You young'ens stop your plunderin'!" from Grandpaw. We would watch him pick up a strange object and ask inquisitively, "What is that, Grandpaw?" "Hit's a layby to ketch meddlers," he would answer dryly. He would spend hours sorting through and looking at the articles in his trunk

We knew that there were many treasures in it. Our imaginations ran wild, surmising just what it did contain. Gold dust, of course—didn't our own father spend some time prospecting out west when he was a young man? Probably some precious stones, maybe pearls, valuable deeds or stocks and bonds—why else was Grandpaw so possessive about it?

We knew that Grandpaw was a collector. During World War II there were many drives to collect various items. Grandpaw collected tinfoil from chewing gum wrappers and cigarette packages. I was a little embarrassed a couple of times when I went to Charleston with him and he would stop on the street, stoop over and retrieve a gum wrapper to add to his collection. He was oblivious to the curious stares of people passing by him; he was serene in the knowledge that his ball of tinfoil was growing. When he turned it in, it weighed several pounds.

Grandpaw collected things around the house, too. Anything that he thought might be useful at some later date, he picked up and squirreled away in his trunk. It was always a source of irritation to my father when he couldn't find a comb when he was getting dressed. He would buy comb after comb but they were nowhere to be found when he needed one. We kids were always getting the blame for losing them. One day when Grandpaw was gone, Daddy looked in his trunk and found seventeen combs stashed away there.

After Grandpaw died, we finally got a chance to examine the things in his mysterious trunk. Eagerly, we dug out his "treasures." There were hundreds of tacks, nails, screws, (mostly used) twine and string wound around sticks and spools. There were shoes for an iron last and an assortment of arrowheads that were commonplace to us. We found them every spring when the garden was plowed. He had saved worn-out shoe heels, empty Prince Albert tobacco cans and Mom's old beads she'd had as a girl. There was a lifetime of odds and ends that were valuable only to Grandpaw.

I still wonder what happened to the treasures in Grandpaw's trunk.

The Charleston Gazette
December 4, 1992

Drifting white clouds float leisurely in a calm blue sky today as August redeems herself and presents us with such beautiful days that the spirit is lightened and the heart is made glad. The recent rain has washed the air clean and sparkling, while a light breeze sways the lavender heads of the Joe-Pye weed and wafts the mellow fragrance of ripe corn tassels through the air. Mornings are reminiscent of early fall, with invigorating cool temperatures and white mist shrouding the mountaintops. This weather makes me want to climb Pilot Knob, or go down on Big Laurel Creek.

I love Clay County. It holds my roots, my childhood, my family, my home and friends and my heart. The ties to home are firm and steadfast, even through the years. Home doesn't have to be an ostentatious dwelling place, with luxurious landscaping and large holdings. It may be a humble hut tucked in the hills, but it is still home. There is no place on earth like it.

Grandpaw was an integral part of my childhood and home. He was there, as long as I can remember. When I was young, he and Grandmaw lived in the old house and we lived in the little house across the yard by the creek. The memories are vague but I remember going up the path between the houses to visit them—which I did several times a day. Grandmaw died when I was only seven and Grandpaw moved in with us and lived there until his death, ten years later.

In my mind, I can see Grandpaw's face plainly and his rather short stature. However, he stood straight as a ramrod and was a man among men. Around the house he wore a blue chambray work shirt and work pants held up by "galluses." It is his Sunday-go-to-meeting clothes that I remember best. He wore old men's high-topped dress shoes, polished shiny and clean, and an old black suit with Sen-Sen in the jacket pocket. I guess the Sen-Sen is what got me to thinking of Grandpaw lately.

Remember Sen-Sen? If you do, it will date you as surely as it did me this week. I called the secretary in the local business office to ask where I could leave a package for UPS. When she told me that Nicholas Pharmacy was a pick-up point, I exclaimed, "Oh, good—I have been wanting to go there to get some Sen-Sen for Mom." There was a puzzled silence, and I asked, "Don't you know what Sen-Sen is?" She giggled and replied, "No-o, is it Biblical?" I explained to her that it is old-timey, tiny squares of chewy, strong licorice that people once used for breath mints. "Oh, I'd hate to go to the drug store and ask for Sen-Sen," she confided. "They might get down and start praying with me!"

To make a long story short, I went to the drug store and inquired about Sen-Sen. The clerk was a good twenty-five years younger than I but she knew what I was talking about. "We did stock it, but we haven't been able to get it for some time," she told me. Then she added, "Yuck—I can't stand that stuff!"

Well, I like it. It was part of my childhood and Grandpaw. I can remember him digging into his coat pocket and sharing it with us, sometimes speckled with lint where it had spilled out of the paper packet. Sen-Sen was as much a part of Grandpaw as his plug of Brown Mule chewing tobacco and store-bought teeth that he wore only on special occasions, and to church. He looked a little strange to us then, as we were used to his toothless gums and pursed mouth.

Grandpaw couldn't read or write and could barely sign his name. This never handicapped his traveling. He loved to visit and would think nothing of boarding a Greyhound bus and jaunting off to Oregon to visit his relatives for a few weeks. He had an old black suitcase that he called a "grip," and when he planned a trip, he would pack it days in advance. Then he would sit on the front porch and wait for the designated person to pick him up. I don't know how he managed changing buses and layovers in strange cities, but he did.

We were always so anxious for his return and he came loaded with little bags of candy and always something special for Mom. He bought her the first pressure cooker we had ever seen. He called it a "steamless cooker," and believe it or not, she is still using it today. It is a heavy model made by Presto and other than replacing the rubber gasket, it has never faltered.

Grandparents are so necessary to children. My maternal grandmother I never knew and I only faintly remember Grandmaw O'Dell. But Grandpaw was special and after 36 years (47 years now), I still miss him. We did so many things together. He loved the fishing trips and always had his gear ready and grip packed long before it was time to go. Cold weather never deterred him, and he would be the first one out and gone in the morning, and the last one back at night.

When anyone in the family planned a fishing trip, he was always ready to go. One time Daddy refused to take him because he had just been discharged from the hospital after having had major surgery and he still had a tube through his stomach wall attached to a gallon jug. After we left and set up our camp on William's River, here came Grandpaw, jug and all. He had called a cousin of mine and talked him into bringing him along.

My most vivid memory of Grandpaw, though, was his whispered prayer after we were all tucked in bed for the night. He slept in the "front" room and we could hear him, after the lights were all turned out, praying in a loud stage whisper, "Lord, we thank Thee for this beautiful 'sunshine day'."

Yes, Grandpaw was special.

The Clay Herald
August 7, 1988

A screech owl called last evening at bedtime, its thin, quavering notes floating out on the evening stillness. It got me to thinking of Old Ed and the booby owls.

Ed appeared on our porch the evening after we had moved, many years ago, to an isolated old farm in Jackson County. He had come to look over his new neighbors who had moved on the old Davis farm that had been vacant for many years. Neighbors were few and far between and Old Ed lived in the most desolate place of all, a little shack deep in the woods beyond our farm.

There he stood, grinning shyly, a weather-beaten old man topped with gray hair and dressed in dirty bib overalls and gumboots. We invited him in for a cup of coffee, which he accepted. After the first sip, he smiled and said, "'Tis better than water, hain't it?" This remark was repeated with glee among us afterwards, but we really didn't know how it was with Old Ed.

He became a daily visitor after that, always eating a meal with us. Ed was a bachelor in his late sixties. He was bashful, yet friendly and much more lonely than we realized at the time. His only love and constant companion was Betty, a mixed beagle that followed him everywhere and lay at his feet in plain adoration.

He worked some on the neighboring farms doing odd jobs when available—shucking corn or cutting fodder. He had worked for some time at fifty cents an hour and one of the farmers there told him one day, "Ed, you've been working good this summer so I am going to give you 75 cents an hour." Ed hitched up the galluses on his overalls, spit a gob of tobacco juice out of the corner of his mouth and blurted, "No-siree-bob, and you hain't a'doin' it neither—if I hain't worth fifty cents an hour, I hain't worth nuthin'!"

The first time he saw me hang laundry out on the line he was plainly shocked, "You're a'ruinin' them kid's clothes a'warshin' them like that. Jist warshes all the color out of them. Look at my overalls," he said, proudly hooking his thumbs around the straps. "When I git a new pair of overalls, I put them on and wear them out—they hain't never warshed." There was no doubt about that. When the wind was right, you could smell Old Ed before he came in sight.

We bought a flock of laying hens from him and the first time they saw me hang wet sheets on the clothesline, they panicked and ran for the woods, squawking and flapping their wings. I guess the sight was as strange to them as it was to Old Ed. Yet, he continued to visit, with faithful Betty at his heels.

On his way to the house, he had to pass through a patch of thick woods where many hoot owls roosted. Ed was leery of the "booby owls," and hated to pass through there. But he would brave the owls in order to make his daily visit. He was fond of our children and when they would amuse him he would slap his leg and roar, "Wal, bust my pitchur!"

One day he came to visit and for the first time, Betty wasn't tagging along. He said Betty was sick and wouldn't eat. The next day he sobbed like a child when he told us that Betty had died. Seemed like the heart went out of Old Ed then. He drooped around and lost his zest for living.

We had a severe cold spell in February that year and one frigid day, Old Ed failed to visit. Another day passed and Criss hitched up our team of black mares to go see about him. He found Old Ed down with pneumonia, barely able to keep a fire going and unable to bring in more firewood.

Criss carried in wood and water for him, then told me later, with tears in his eyes, about Old Ed's living conditions. He had a bed made of poles laced with grass rope and stuffed with gunnysacks. A horse collar and harness hung on the wall above a rickety table. A battered dresser and a worn-out chair made up the rest of his furniture. There was no food in the house. We hadn't dreamed that he was so terribly poor. That one meal a day that he ate with us was all the food he had.

Criss made a trip each day with the horses, taking care of him until he recovered. Then he took him to a lawyer to apply for his veteran's benefits—Ed was a WWI veteran. I'll never forget the first check that he received. It was about a ten-mile hike to the country store and Old Ed came back with a bulging gunnysack on his back. Every five or six-feet there was a discarded banana peeling behind him. Old Ed was living high on the hog.

We moved back to Clay County soon after that and later we heard that Ed's health had gone downhill. After a severe illness he was admitted to the Veteran's Hospital in Huntington. He lived there the remainder of his days. We saw him one time after he went to the hospital to live and he seemed happy as he described the good food and pretty nurses. And he was safe from the booby owls.

The Clay Herald
May 13, 1991

The Charleston Gazette
May 21, 1991

I told my Aunt Lucy good-bye on a cold, snow-shrouded day right after Christmas. Many times in the past we had bid one another farewell but this time it was final.

She is mingled in my earliest memories. She married my Uncle Myles the same year that I was born, and as far back as I can remember, they were a vital part of our lives.

Uncle Myles was my father's younger brother and unlike Mom and Dad, who began producing offspring every whipstitch, he and Aunt Lucy were childless for many years. As a result, they practically adopted us children as their own. They made their home in South Charleston, while we stayed on the old home place in Clay County. Their frequent visits were one of the highlights of our days.

In memory, I see Aunt Lucy as she looked then. Thin as a rail, with hair as black as a crow, she was a foil for the handsome manliness of Uncle Myles. They never came without bringing gifts for each one of the children. I remember Uncle Myles striding up the path to our house, his face beaming with the wide, familiar smile, holding out his arms for the bear hug that he always gave us. Aunt Lucy toted us around on her sharp hipbone—and she always had one of us on her hip. It was like Christmas every time they came.

Christmas was another thing. With no children to buy for, they bought for us instead. She must have carefully selected the gifts throughout the year, for they would come bearing a huge cardboard box of individually wrapped presents for all of us. Aunt Lucy was one of those rare people who always wanted to help someone else.

Their little house in South Charleston is gone now, swallowed up by the interstate highway. It stands out plainly in memory, though, amid a row of like houses crouched between Kanawha Turnpike and the railroad tracks. We spent a lot of time there, especially during the summer months when there was no school. Long ago faces and names come to mind: Mrs. Smith, "Toots" Mayes, Mabel Harris—many of them gone, just as the street itself is no more.

Sometimes we would grow a bit homesick for farm life while we were visiting there and the lonesome wail of the freight trains passing the house in the night would awaken an answering cry from us. I remember playing a wartime record on the old phonograph, the words cutting like a knife through my homesickness, "Good-bye my love/It's time to go/I heard the silver trumpet blow/It's calling me to fight the foe/good-bye my love, good-bye." I wept bitterly.

It was a treat to visit there and even more so after the children came. I can still see the pride and joy when baby Kay came into their lives when I was ten years old. She was almost the same age as my sister Jeannie and Aunt Lucy and Mom would jokingly compare Jeannie's fair looks and blonde hair with Kay's darker complexion and reddish-brown hair that curled slightly. "Every old crow thinks her little crow is the blackest," Aunt Lucy would say smugly.

Jimmy was added to their household and their family was complete. Jimmy would spend a week here at the farm with my brother Larry, amid cows and chickens that were strange to him. Before the week was up, he would complain that "there was nothing to do." Larry would return the visit to town and despite the luxury of an indoor bathroom and the LaBelle theater, he would be fretting after a few days that "there's nothing to do." They were a true case of the city mouse and the country mouse.

On down through the years, our lives mingled. I lived with them for two years before I was married and it was to their house that I brought our first-born son, Michael. His first night was spent in Aunt Lucy's dresser drawer before we came on home the next day. She was with me when Andy was born—it seemed that she was always there when we needed her.

When Criss and I fell upon hard times in Jackson County, she and Uncle Myles made many weekend trips with a load of groceries. She confided to me later that those trips were among some of the happiest times of their marriage. We would build a big fire in the wood stove, pop corn, and listen to the wind howl around the farmhouse, while icicles would freeze from the roof to the ground. We were warm and safe inside.

Aunt Lucy never asked much out of life other than to help someone else. She was the one to fix, mend, or repair whatever was needed. Yet, she wasn't perfect by any means. She had a quick temper and a sharp tongue that she used on occasion. The sharp side of her tongue was never turned on me, however. She was good to everyone who would permit her.

The years went by and we told them good-bye when Uncle Myles was transferred to the Taft plant in Louisiana. After he retired, they came back to South Charleston for a short time. We told them good-bye again when Aunt Lucy's health began failing and they moved to Georgia to live with their daughter Kay.

Aunt Lucy passed away on Christmas Day. It hurts to say good-bye for the last time.

The Charleston Gazette
January 7, 1994

The Clay County Free Press
January 12, 1994

Her brown eyes twinkle behind her eyeglasses and a dimple flashes in and out as she talks. It is hard to believe that she will celebrate her 93rd (now 96th) birthday this month.

Della White Summers is Ovapa's oldest resident and still an active lady. She keeps house for one of her sons, Oral, where she cooks three hot meals each day. She admits that she has slowed down the last couple of years, though and she hasn't done any garden work since then.

"Yes, you have, Mom," Oral corrects her. "Last summer I found your tracks in the garden where you had set out some plants." She giggles as she recalls, "Yes, I did. I raise my own plants and they weren't set out to suit me. I went along the row and pulled out some and reset them."

Her hands are busy over an oval quilting frame as she works on a handmade quilt. "I just can't stand to sit," she confides, as she looks around the cozy living room. "Used to be, before Thanksgiving, I would take all my curtains down, wash and starch them stiff and stretch them on curtain stretchers so my house would look nice. I can't do things like that now."

It is easy to see that she has always been an industrious person and she has had a busy summer. She and daughter Lola canned over 80 quarts of green beans, froze and pickled corn, made pickles and kraut. It is not a drop in the bucket to what she used to put up for the winter.

She and her husband Pat, who passed away in 1974, raised nine children on this Clay County farm. They had ten, but one died in infancy. Her voice grows pensive as she recalls tiny Arthur Allen. "He got sick one day with a bad diarrhea and we couldn't get him over it. We took him to the doctor and he told me if I could, to take the whey off buttermilk and try to get some down him." She adds with sadness, "He died in my arms the next morning."

All her children were born at home except the youngest, Ronnie, who was born in Staats Hospital. She was 44 year old and had developed a heart condition. She begged Dr. Quick of Clendenin to deliver her at home. He told her, "I am not about to attempt a home delivery without oxygen, and a bunch of granny women standing around wringing their hands." The matter was taken out of her hands when she had two heart attacks as she went into labor and three afterward.

At 93, her health is fairly good, although she is on medication for her heart and blood pressure. Her hearing is good and her mind is sharp. She has almost a century of memories stored there.

She was born at Wanego, on Grannies Creek before there was a post office at Ovapa. John Waddy Westfall carried the mail on horseback from Camp Creek to Pigeon in Roane County, then on to Wanego. She and her husband lived there during the early years of their marriage. She said that they moved so many times during that period that the chickens would lay down and cross their legs to be tied. The Ovapa Post Office, which was established the same year that she was married, was located in the Ira Brown store.

She has seen many changes in Ovapa since that time. There was no road then; the creek bed was traveled by vehicles. The area was farming land, with cleared fields and livestock. Farm families kept horses, cattle, hogs and chickens. Housewives had to rely heavily on home remedies for their illnesses and injuries and "granny women" delivered most of their babies. She had quite a surprise when her fifth baby was born.

That day, she had gone to a company picnic at Huntington with her family and when she got home that evening, she realized that the baby was coming early. Dr. Smith was out on another call, but Dr. Goad happened to be at her brother Walter's house delivering their first baby, June. He came on up the holler and soon delivered her of a fine baby boy.

He asked her how she was feeling and she replied, "Well, I've got a bad pain in my side." He examined her, and with a funny look on his face, he commented, "Well, I hope you've got another set of baby clothes!" In a little while, there was a second baby boy. They are the twins, Elbert and Delbert.

With twenty-eight grandchildren and twenty-nine (almost thirty, she says) great-grandchildren, she is still called upon for some of her home remedies. She mixes "granny grease" with lard (use a right smart of lard, she cautions)lamp oil, turpentine and camphor or camphorated oil. This is good for chest colds, congestion and can be rubbed on the back for backaches. She gathered pennyroyal and made tea for colds, and made onion tea for a sleep aid.

An onion poultice was good for chest congestion and a near neighbor, Maw Braley, taught her to rub the bottoms of a baby's feet with the grease the onions were fried in for a chest cold.

With her gray hair pulled back in a granny knot (it has never been cut) she is the epitome of an old-fashioned grandmother. She looks around at the framed pictures and snapshots of her family and says softly, "The Lord has been good to me to allow me to live all these years. I have had a good life, good neighbors and a good family."

The family is scattered some now but a lot of them live fairly close to home. Lola Rogers and Charlotte Jett live a stone's throw away at Valley Fork.

Oral is still at home, Delbert is at Ivydale and Jimmy is here and there, as he is a longhaul truck driver. The others are in Ohio, with Arnold Ray at Akron, Norma Jean Colcamp at Magodore and Elbert and Ronnie both living at Hartville.

     You can be sure though, as
Thanksgiving rolls around that all
those who can make it will be home.

                    The Charleston Gazette
                    November 22, 1996

                    The Clay County Free Press
                    November 27, 1996

     May is weeping. Green tears fall
on greener fields, on dripping dogwood
blossoms, on Mayapple umbrellas. Fronds
of weeping willow sway back and forth
and a cold mist worries the brow of the
hilltops. Rain falls sadly on fading
trillium blossoms, in dark and woodsy
hollows and patters on trees that are
growing green and leafy.
     My heart echoes the sad drip of
the rain. My Aunt May is gone, passed
away on this Mayday in the faraway
state of Oregon. She was homesick for
the hills and never failed in each
letter back home to mention that "it is
beautiful here but it's not home and I
miss my friends back East."
     I had the sinking feeling when she
told us good-bye on the day that she
left a couple of years ago that we'd
never see her again. It had come as a
surprise earlier when she revealed that
she was moving to the West Coast with
her daughter and son-in-law, after

living all her life in the eastern region. She had been in poor health for some time and wanted to spend her remaining days near her only surviving granddaughter, who lived in Oregon.

It was a wrench to see her go, to pull up stakes and relocate clear across the country. She gave to us many of her treasured things and everywhere I look, there is a remembrance of her—a plaque that belonged to her deceased granddaughter, flower prints in pastel hues and numerous household items.

She knew me before I ever recognized her. She was a witness to my birth, down on the waters of Big Laurel Creek. Grandma O'Dell delivered me, as the doctor didn't get there in time. Aunt May was right there to welcome me into the world. Mom had a recurring fear that her first-born child would look like a crawdab, with eyes set too close to her nose. Aunt May took her first look and remarked, "Well, she's pretty but her eyes are too far apart!"

Aunt May had humble country beginnings. Born to Daddy's brother Walter and Fanny (Holcomb) O'Dell, her mother died when she was only a few days old. Grandma O'Dell was expecting her last child, Uncle Myles, at the time and she took her granddaughter to raise.

Grandma would tie the milk cow to the front gate at night, in order to get up and obtain warm milk when the baby got hungry. When Uncle Myles was born six months later, she breast-fed both of them. She was always called "sister" by Daddy and Uncle Myles and as Uncle Myles once stated, "You can't get any closer than that!"

Aunt May married, had one daughter, Mary Leta and later divorced and left the country behind. She put herself through beauty school and became a hairdresser. My earliest memories of her are enmeshed with the beauty shop on Quarrier Street and the permanents she generously gave us girls.

Aunt May was the epitome of glamour to us, in contrast to our sedate country life. My sisters and I all stayed with her from time to time and I lived with her part of the time when I graduated from high school. A flaming redhead, she was intolerant of any type of prejudice and what she termed "narrow-minded thinking." Her language was as colorful as her character and her rather flamboyant lifestyle was often viewed askance by Daddy. She opened her heart and home to us, fixed our hair, let us wear her expensive clothes and loved us. We, in turn, loved her.

So many, many memories flit through my mind—the house at Rand with her English husband, Uncle Frank and the red raspberries in the back yard and fat asparagus spears that grew in the garden. I remember the kindness shown to us by Uncle Frank and how generous and loving they both were.

Although she traveled abroad quite a bit, lived in England for some time and settled in Reston, Virginia, during her later years, she made periodic visits home. She loved the country food of home and Mom always tried to fix "leather britches" (fodder beans) or fresh half runners when she visited.

In failing health for several years, she still dressed in fashionable clothes (which she often passed on down to us) and kept her hair styled and youthful. We were always so glad to see her as she swept in on a cloud of expensive perfume and enveloped us in an exuberant hug and gave us a hearty kiss.

Her last request was in keeping with her lifestyle—that her body be cremated and the ashes sprinkled in the Pacific Ocean.

I can visualize them floating out to sea, drawn up in vaporous clouds by the sun, blown hither and yon by the wind, to settle to earth again in weeping rain drops. I like to think that a few of them will return to the hills, to rest in the land of her birth.

The Charleston Gazette
May 5, 1995

The Clay County Free Press
May 12, 1995

Uncle Clarence Brown was a fine neighbor. He wasn't really our uncle but as he was kin to more than half of the folks on Summer's Fork, we called him uncle also.

He lived right below us while I was growing up, across from the post office and general store. His yard bordered the dirt road and was enclosed by a fence that confined his dog, Trouble. "Trouble Brown, meanest dog in town," he would tell us. I don't think he would have been that mean if the kids hadn't teased him on their way to Hagar School, kicking the fence and setting him to snarling and barking.

Uncle Clarence seemed old as far back as I can remember. He was always ready to lend a helping hand, as country neighbors are prone to do. I remember one time, right after Criss and I were married, that we were trying to get some newly harvested hay in the barn before a threatening thunderstorm approached. Uncle Clarence grabbed a pitchfork and began throwing piles of hay up in the barn for Criss and me to store. I have never forgotten that neighborly concern.

He did have one besetting weakness, however—a love for the bottle. When he was in his cups, he was a different person. His long-suffering wife, Mary, took it all in stride and bore with it. He would stretch out in the yard after he reached a certain stage and yell loudly, "Yah, Pete

Dillinger!" All the nearby neighbors knew that Uncle Clarence had gotten hold of a bottle.

Sometimes he would call to his wife, "Hey, Mary-Pete!" She would ignore him and go on about her business. One evening he lay in the yard until dark. Mary went on to bed and soon a summer shower of rain passed overhead. She said she heard him crawl up on the porch.

He would often hire someone to take him to Clay to purchase a bottle and other times he would hitchhike. Many times he would get down beside the road before he got home. I can see him now, half-lying beside the road with his thumb extended, hoping for a ride.

He had another problem, too. Whoever picked him up had trouble getting him out of their vehicle when they got him home. He would turn stubborn and refuse to budge.

One day we were coming up the holler when we spied Uncle Clarence sitting beside the road, thumbing his way home. Daddy was driving a pickup truck and he was hauling a rocking chair in the back. He stopped and said, "Clarence, the cab is full,(of Mom and young'ens) but you can ride in the back if you want to."

Uncle Clarence climbed up in the bed of the truck and we started on up the road. Daddy looked back and saw Uncle Clarence rocking merrily in the rocking chair. When we got almost home, a dog ran out in front of the truck and Daddy had to make a quick stop. The rocking chair upended in a tangle of legs and rockers and Uncle Clarence came crawling out from underneath the chaos. That was one time we didn't have any problem getting him to vacate a vehicle.

They were an important part of our childhood—Uncle Clarence and Mary and granddaughter Margaret Ann, whom they raised. Clarence and Mary are both gone, of course, but rich memories still linger. Sometimes in the twilight I can almost hear the old cry, "Yah, Pete Dillinger!"

* * * * * * *

When Criss and I were first married, we had another neighbor with the same weakness. One day we got a call from a state policeman, asking Criss if he had such a neighbor. When Criss told him yes, he asked if he would come and get his horse and bring it home. It seemed that he had been arrested for "drunken riding" and was being taken to the county jail. Of course they couldn't arrest the horse, so he told the policeman to call Criss to come after it.

When Criss got there, the horse had been tied to a signpost, still garbed in its harness. It was a tall work horse and Criss couldn't mount it. He led it up the dirt road toward home and when he reached a high bank, he jumped on its back. The horse had a weakness too. The harder you pulled on its reins, the faster he would go.

It was a wild and woolly ride across Hoppy's Hill, with Criss hollering and trying to stop the steed. When they crossed the bridge at the Methodist Church, he jumped off and limped the rest of the way home (Criss limped, not the horse). He said the next time that it happened, they could take the horse to jail too.

* * * * * * * *

My brother Mark was always a different kid. He was the one, whenever a family snapshot was taken, who stuck out his tongue or made an ugly face for the camera.

Perhaps it was because he was the middle child in our family of seven children, that he felt the need to assert himself. Coming after the first three children and followed closely by younger brother Ronnie, he had to become a scrapper to establish his place in the family.

Or it could have been because he had an eye that tended to wander toward his nose, until it was corrected by eyeglasses, that caused him to always play the clown. He broke his glasses regularly and they were nearly always held together by a piece of black tape. His hair was thick and stubby and the summer sun would bleach it out almost white.

As the oldest in the family, it became my job to give all the kids their Saturday night bath. All through the week, we did our absolutions in a tin wash pan, but on Saturday night the old No. 3 wash tub was unhooked from its nail on the side of the house and pressed into service.

This was not a simple procedure by any means. Water had to be pumped from the pitcher pump in front of the Virginia office building, carried in zinc water buckets to the house and then heated on the cooking stove. No wonder it was a once a week ritual.

Larry and Mary Ellen were old enough to take their own baths but the four younger ones were my responsibility. I remember scrubbing Mark down from head to foot, then pouring water over his head to rinse his hair. He had a crooked, appealing grin that melted your heart.

Time went on, we both grew up and married, then eventually settled down with our families on family land. For many years, we lived in sight of one another. It seemed that life would always go on in this manner, everyday living and normal routine, our lives touching, merging, and flowing onward. Sometimes change comes so suddenly that it takes us by surprise and we are unprepared. Then, perhaps we are never prepared for change.

Mark worked away a lot, coming home many times just for the weekend. He always found time to drop in and visit for a spell. Sunday morning usually found him at the kitchen door with his coffee cup. He'd always greet me with a "Hi, Girl!" and we'd visit while I cooked breakfast.

He was always the compassionate one, ready to take up for the underdog. My own children would turn to him when they needed help or advice and he would show such understanding and concern. You could confide anything to him and know that it would go no farther.

In late November of 1997, he began experiencing severe pain in his back. Since he'd had disc problems and back surgery before, the doctor suspected a slipped disc and admitted him to the hospital where he was put in traction. In just a few days, tests revealed cancer cells in his blood.

He was then transferred to Charleston Memorial's Oncology Unit, where a suspicious lesion on a rib was found. The doctor began an aggressive campaign against the cancer, with radiation and chemotherapy. Mark weighed 174 pounds when the treatments began.

His life then consisted of a round of treatments, hospital admissions, blood transfusions and pain. By early spring, he weighed less than a hundred pounds and was a blackened hull of a man. The thick thatch of hair was gone, he was being fed through a tube in his stomach and a central line was inserted in the vein of his neck. He could barely creep through the house on a walker but the cheerful, crooked grin was still there.

One morning I went into his bedroom and he was barely holding on to life. He told me, "Alyce Faye, it was not supposed to be like this." I tried to comfort him. Then he added in a faint whisper, "I'm giving it up."

I sunk to my knees and began crying, "Oh, Mark, you can't," I sobbed. "You're not saved." He told me humbly, "I don't deserve to be saved." I answered him, "Mark, none of us deserve to be saved." Then I asked him if he wanted me to pray with him and I prayed a heartbroken prayer.

The next day, my sister Mary Ellen and our pastor went up to visit him and Mark was saved.

He rallied some after that and attended services at church a few times. With much effort, he would make his way to the front pew, assisted by a cane or a walker. He would testify to the goodness of God and how God in His mercy had forgiven Mark and made him one of His own children. There would not be a dry eye in the congregation when he finished.

An acquaintance dropped in on a Sunday service when Mark gave his testimony. He stopped by our house after service and remarked, "I felt so sorry for that old gentleman who talked in the service." I asked him, "Just how old do you think that old gentleman was?" He answered, "Oh, probably in his eighties." I told him, "That old gentleman is my brother and he is 56 years old." The man was shocked.

In May 1998, God took Mark home. We had known of his illness barely six months—there was not enough time to even get used to the idea that he was sick. We were all around his bedside, his wife and children, his brothers and sisters. Mom was holding his hand when he took his last breath.

I miss him most on Sunday morning. I can almost see him stick his head in the kitchen door, coffee cup in hand, and say, "Hi, Girl!" Some day, I'll hear him say it again.

* * * * * * * *

Like all country places, we had our share of unforgettable characters. We had one old bachelor named John that lived in the neighborhood all my growing-up days and longer. We kids sort of shunned him, as he was an extremely dirty, smelly old man.

I don't know where he came from but he lived alone in an old shack up on a hill and wandered through the neighborhood day after day. I guess the grown-ups tolerated him, as I remember

Daddy cutting his hair(and cleaning the clippers thoroughly afterward!).

He couldn't see well and would squint up his eyes when looking at an object. He carried a staff to help him walk, and wore an old black hat winter and summer. We tried to stay away from him as far as possible.

He bit his fingernails into the quick and his dirty hands were particularly repugnant. As our children grew up, they too shied away from him.

One day he was standing on Opal's general store porch eating out of a box of oyster crackers. Kevin was about five years old and he wandered by just then. John gave Kevin the box of crackers and off he took with them. Patty was watching them and she was scandalized. She took after Kevin like a hen after a June bug and he ran up in the woods, cramming the crackers in his mouth as fast as he could.

When she caught him, she took the crackers from him and came to the house boiling mad. "John had been eating out of that box with his old dirty hands," she raged. Kevin didn't care—he wanted the crackers.

My neighbor Mildred told me something then that made me stop and think. "I wonder if anyone prays for John?" she asked me. I had never thought about it. He was a soul also, in spite of his appearance and personality. Now, I try to consider each person I meet as one of God's

creations, in spite of their
shortcomings.

* * * * * * * *

I guess we have always had
colorful characters in these hills. I
remember Grandpa O'Dell telling of a
man that worked for him in the woods.
His name was Enoch Lanham and they were
cutting trees on a logging job. The day
grew late and Enoch got tired. He sat
down on a log and called from time to
time, as if his crew was felling a
tree, "Watch her go down, boys!"
Grandpa sneaked up on him just as he
called out again and asked mildly,
"Watch what go down, Enoch?" Enoch
replied in a flash, "That evening sun!"

Unpublished

CHAPTER FOUR

SIMMERING SUMMERTIME DAYS

> "Christ Jesus, when I come to
> die
> Grant me a clean, sweet
> summer sky,
> Without the mad wind's
> panther cry.
> Send me a little garden
> breeze
> To gossip in magnolia trees."
> ...Hervey Allen

The rain began softly in the night, a muted insistent murmur of sound that gradually intruded on our consciousness. It was an unfamiliar sound after so many weeks of dry weather, but so welcome. It had thundered a couple of times before we went to bed but we were almost afraid to hope that it was the portent of impending rain.

We lay in bed with grateful hearts and listened to the patter of rain on the roof and could imagine the tiny roots of the plants and grass greedily absorbing the life-giving moisture. The bosom of the earth was once more giving sustenance to all the green and growing things.

It continued steadily into the morning, a light but constant offering of moisture, then tapered off, leaving the humidity behind. There is a fresh greenness to the trees and underbrush and the gardens seem to have taken a new lease on life. Little puddles of water have formed along the road and the bone-dry ditch is running again. It wasn't enough, of course; it will take days and nights of steady rain to alleviate the dryness of our land. Still, it helped and we are thankful.

I remember how glad we were as kids when we would get a rainy day at this time of the year. It seemed as if we spent days hoeing corn, tedious row after row, with the hot sun baking our heads and the sweat bees taking a toll out of our hides. We used to put the whole bottom in field corn and it would take the better part of a week to hoe the whole patch.

Mornings weren't too bad, starting early while the air was cool and we were fresh and energetic. Along about ten o'clock, however, the sun would beat down hotter and hotter and the rows seemed to get longer and longer. Sand briers would attack our bare feet, and those pesky sweat bees would crawl up under an armpit or the back of your neck and test your fortitude. After you mashed the first one, it would excite them into a fury and then you would get attacked. When it seemed you were about to die of thirst, or heat, or exhaustion, Mom would holler that it was time for dinner.

Remember that summertime food? New creamed potatoes and fresh peas, wilted lettuce and green onions, homemade cottage cheese and hot cornbread dripping with cow butter. We worked hard and we could put away the food. All too soon, our hour's respite was over and it was back to the cornfield.

The afternoon was murder. The sun shone down with a vengeance and muscles grew sore and tired. We would hoe until suppertime and then fall into bed early, totally exhausted. After a few days of hoeing, no wonder we welcomed a rainy day.

Oh, that was a good feeling to awaken to the sound of rain drumming on the roof and know that there would be no hoeing corn that day! I usually used the time to curl up with a good book and read all day long. Sometimes Mary Ellen and I would play with paper dolls—dolls that we drew ourselves and we also designed their clothes. Rainy days were good for telling stories and playing guessing games or "I Spy." With seven kids in our family, there was always a gang to play.

One of the best things about this time of year, though, were the green apples. Like all country kids, we were cautioned about eating green apples "because they will give you the bellyache." You know, I don't ever remember really having a bellyache from eating them. And I ate my share. We had two apple trees up in the end of the garden and when the corn was knee high or so, Mom couldn't see us from the house. With a salt shaker hidden in our pocket, Larry and I would make a beeline for the earliest apple tree, which also happened to have a low limb that was handy to climb. There we would sit and pluck and eat green apples to our heart's content.

One day I climbed up first, as Larry was having a little trouble shinnying up the tree. He picked up a rotten log that was under the tree and braced it on the tree trunk. Unknown to either of us, there was a yellow jacket nest in the log, and they were furious at being disturbed. Larry discovered them before he climbed the tree and ran as fast as his legs could carry him. However, I was already up the tree and trapped. I got stung so many times that I finally chanced a broken leg and jumped anyway.

I paid for those green apples. My feet and legs swelled so badly that it was days before I could walk normally. Naturally, Mom knew why we were in the apple tree but she didn't say too much. I guess she figured that we had been punished amply. Larry was stung all over too.

Jeannie and Susie were a little more devious. They would take a supply of green apples to the barn, along with the necessary salt shaker. There they would feast without fear of being discovered. One day Mom happened to climb up in the barn loft and there she found a whole row of salt shakers that had been squirreled away over a period of time.

Sometimes I feel guilty when I run the grandchildren away from a little semi-dwarf apple tree that has less than a half dozen apples on it, simply because I want to see what kind of apples they are when they mature. I remember what a good time we had as kids sneaking and eating the forbidden fruit.

It almost makes me wish that I could climb the old apple tree again

(with a salt shaker of course) and eat
all the green apples I could hold.

The Clay Herald
July 18, 1988

Summer explodes in our hills with
resulting heat, humidity and long, hazy
days. The roadsides and fields are
adorned with the gayest of
flowers—bold black-eyed Susans,
flamboyant orange pleurisy weed and day
lilies of a softer orange hue, standing
with regal heads on long, slender
stems. The milkweed, with its floppy
head and sweet, cloying fragrance,
exudes a sticky fluid, while the white
blossoms on the elderberry have given
way to hard, green berries.

Summer simmers along, while out in
the fields the blackberries have
ripened. There are so many good natural
foods here in the hills, if a person
knows where to harvest them, and how to
prepare them afterward.

That reminds me of a recent James
Dent column, which dwelt with the
characteristics of a true mountaineer.
While I have no quarrel with the
findings, it seemed to me that it was a
discourse prepared for males by males.

The true mountaineer woman also
has some distinguishing earmarks. It's

not "Can she bake a cherry pie, Billy Boy," or even "Can she bake a blackberry cobbler, Billy Bob?" (I know women who have never dwelt in these hills who can make a lovely cobbler.) But one true test of a born and bred hill woman is if she can cook a groundhog. While it takes a true mountain man to catch the groundhog, don't rule out the woman in this venture.

I recall an instance in my girlhood, when I brought a beau home to introduce to the family and Mom had gone on a hunting expedition of her own. She and some of my brothers were hoeing corn when the dog holed something on the hill above them. Grabbing a mattock and a hoe, she hurried to the site to dig out supper. It was a subdued bunch, with a definite "air" about them, that greeted me and the prospective boy friend, when we pulled into the driveway. It seemed the groundhog was a black creature, with a white stripe down the back. The beau must have been impressed—I never saw him again. I don't care—he wasn't mountaineer material anyway.

A real mountaineer must have a good hunting dog and my own expert tells me that the best groundhog dog is one that learns to tree a groundhog rather than hole one. He says that when a person is hard-up and sorta puny and hungry, it is a sight easier to shake one out of a tree than to dig one out of a hole.

After the main course is captured, a real mountain woman knows how to cook it (You have to plan ahead with this meal—it starts the day before).

After the animal is skinned and dressed, cut it into serving size pieces. Be sure and remove the kernels under each leg—this is important to remove the "gamey" taste. Soak the groundhog overnight in cold water with a handful of coarse salt.

The next day, drain off the water, then parboil in fresh water with a few twigs of spicewood bush. (This is another test. A true mountain woman knows how to identify spicewood and where to gather it.) In case spicewood is not available, you can use a tablespoon or so of pickling spice or a slug of vinegar in the cooking water. I have used both together.

Cook for approximately an hour, then drain and wash pot and groundhog. Place back in cooker with fresh water, and add a potato, a carrot, a small onion and a stalk of celery. Add salt to taste, and cook until tender. The meat can then be rolled in flour and fried in hot fat until crusty brown, or placed in a pan, brushed with butter or bacon grease and browned in the oven. A young groundhog can be fried in the same manner as chicken after it has soaked overnight.

There are many outstanding traits in a mountain woman but it is in the culinary field that she excels. She is an expert in making a good meal out of very little. (A relative of mine from another state was heard to remark, during the Great Depression, "Those people from West Virginia will never starve—they eat stewed weeds!")

Wild greens do abound and after the poke greens are gone, there are still pursley (purslane) and lamb's quarter. Wild raspberries, huckleberries and blackberries are there for the picking and elderberries make lovely jelly. The true mountain woman eats "soakies" for a snack (richly creamed coffee poured over a hot, buttered biscuit) and relishes grits with her sausage and eggs for breakfast. These new-fangled disposable diapers amaze her; the "hippens" she used were cloth and completely re-cyclable.

The true mountain woman is resourceful and versed in the art of "make do" and "wear out." She is hopelessly outnumbered and a vanishing breed. There are still a few around.

The Clay Herald
July 1, 1991

The Charleston Gazette
August 8, 1991

The leaves hang limp and dusty in the hot July sun and there seems to be no relief in sight for the heat wave that is enveloping our country. The moisture seems to be wrung out from the very air itself, and the soil is dry and dusty. The common little white clover blossoms are brown and crispy underfoot, with lawns and fields also brown and sere. Some flowers struggle valiantly to bloom, with the hardy Queen Anne's lace and black-eyed Susans appearing in the fields and along roadsides. Spots of bright orange reveal butterfly weed or pleurisy root and the white, starry flowers of the curved plume of the lizard's tail hangs over the creek.

Along the creeks and bottoms, the elderberry bushes are white with bloom, and blackberries are hard and green. Lack of rain will most likely affect the berry harvest, as well as garden produce and other foods. The searing heat affects us humans as well and our main desire is to seek out a shady spot to find relief. My mind goes back as to how we whiled away hot summertime days when we were kids.

For one thing, the heat never seemed to bother us too much. There were never enough hours in the day to do all the things that we wanted to do and we always had some project going. I remember one summer when we dug up the chicken lot looking for an Indian grave. (Well, it looked like an Indian mound!) Children nowadays, with all the planned activities and sophisticated toys, will still moan at times that "there's nothing to do!"

We had plenty to do. Of course, we worked hard too—hoeing in the garden, picking blackberries, minding babies and putting up hay when we were older— yet, there was still time to play. Extremely hot days would find us playing in or near the creek, which was much larger then and a whole lot cleaner. We had a clay mud bank near a big rock that yielded hours of making pottery dishes and vases, not to mention beautiful mud cakes and pies.

The younger girls had playhouses in the most unlikely places. Susie and Doris King had one under our house and Mary Ellen and Janice Carole built one in Lovel's chicken house. The woods were one of our very favorite places. We would spend hours there climbing trees and bending them down to the ground, playing cowboys and Indians and making mossy playhouses. Perhaps we were tomboys, but the girls were as daring as the boys and grew strong and athletic.

I'll never forget an incident that happened when Larry and I were pretty small. We had a couple of trees near the house that were our particular favorites. We would climb the bigger tree to the top, bend it down into the top of the smaller one and grasp it, then ride the second one on down to the ground.

There was a snag on the second tree that stuck out six or eight inches from the top and on one of my return journeys to the earth, I twisted my body around and that short limb hooked me in the back of the collar. I turned loose of the first tree and there I hung, suspended between heaven and earth.

I hollered as loudly as I could with the wind being choked out of me and Larry danced around the tree, clapping his hands and chortling with laughter. I guess it finally dawned on him that I was really choking to death and he went to the house and got Mom. She plucked me off the tree, with stern instructions to "be careful climbing around," but of course, as soon as she was out of sight, we were scrambling back up and swinging down again.

There were quiet times when we played games and we read a lot. At the risk of being labeled "aged," (James Dent called the ones who could remember the Katzenjammer Kids "old-timers"), I remember the comic strips that we enjoyed as kids. I read "Smilin' Jack" faithfully—remember him? And Fat Stuff and the scrawny chicken that followed him around and gobbled up the shirt buttons that popped off his ample chest? "Terry and the Pirates" were one of my favorites and I would rush home from school to catch the radio program featuring this adventurer and his lovely ladies—Dragon Lady, for one. I grew up with "Li'l Abner" and his family of Pansy and Pappy Yokum, Tiny and Daisy Mae. I was too young to appreciate his underlying commentary of our government but the characters were colorful and entertaining even to a kid.

There were Senator Phogbound (good old Jack S.), Marryin' Sam, Sadie Hawkins, Wolf Gal, and many, many more. They don't draw cartoon characters now like they used to.

And those radio programs—they were so clean and interesting. Remember Dagwood and Blondie, with the regular characters of Digby O'Dell (old Digger H., the friendly undertaker,) and Mrs. Buff Orphington, and her big, long limousine? Then there was Henry Aldrich the perennial adolescent. I can still hear his mother calling, "Henry-Henry Aldrich!" And his squeaky answer, "Coming, Mother!"

Our whole family liked Baby Snooks, who was sponsored by the makers of Jello. Remember the jingle, "Just a taste of tempting Jello, and believe me you will know, it's the one and only J-E-L-L-O!" Then Baby Snooks sniggered, "Heh-heh-I like it!"

My all time favorite, however, was Pogo Possum and his southern friends deep in the Okeefenokee Swamp. I used to buy every issue of Pogo Comics that came out, so I could keep up with Albert Alligator and all the rest. Yes, those were the good old days!

The Clay Herald
July 11, 1988

Rain continues to fall relentlessly across our hills and hollers this morning, filling the creeks to overflowing with swirling, muddy water. Brown puddles of water stand in the garden patches, where the weeds are growing faster than the plants. In many low-lying areas, the creeks and streams have swelled out of their banks and cover the roadways. Rain continues to fall with monotonous, insistent dripping upon full-leafed trees and fast-growing grasses. It runs off the hillsides in swift rivulets, adding to the swollen creeks and rushing onward to the rising rivers.

These are not one of the sudden, soft showers of summer, when the sun pops out behind the rain and dries the fresh-washed earth. It is not the usual thunderstorm that growls and threatens, then drenches the ground in a sudden downpour and moves on. This has been a steady, day-in, day-out rain that wears on the nerves and makes you long for a glimpse of the sun once more.

I used to love to play in the barn on rainy summer days. We would burrow back in the sweet-smelling hay like a litter of small woodland animals hiding in a haystack. There we would play, snug and cozy, while the rain made a steady drumming on the tin roof.

Sometimes I would sneak off alone with an engrossing book, and spend hours reading and listening to the hypnotic beat of the rain.

Other times, we would retreat to our corn crib play house and play all afternoon while the rain made music on its tin roof. There, shut in from the world by the rain, we had our own private world. Sometimes we pretended that the corn crib was a ship a-sail on the ocean and we sailed through the whitecapped waves safe and sound. Other times it was an Indian teepee and the rain resounded on the buffalo hide walls while we savages crouched around a pretend campfire and roasted strips of venison on the end of a stick.

Occasionally, we pretended that we were shut in a little log cabin deep in the heart of a vast forest and we had to live off the land and our own wits. We would scavenge the surrounding area for our food, a handful of dewberries or a dozen or so small wild strawberries. We would dig a potato or two out of Daddy's potato patch or pick a bunch of tender mountain tealeaves. It was the rule that we couldn't get anything from the house, so after we were thoroughly soaked to the skin, we would crawl back in the corn crib and divide our bounty. The pretending grew so real that we actually felt famished and ate greedily.

When the rain was warm we played right out in it. Splashing barefoot through mud puddles was great fun. The rain soaked through our hair, ran down our faces in rivulets, and wet us through and through. We would stand in the drip of the house and let the rain pour over us in a gushing stream. Sometimes we would shampoo our hair and rinse it in the "drip" of the house. Often the rain would stop before we finished and we would have to stick our heads in Mom's tubs of wash water and suffer the consequences.

When we lived in Jackson County in the old two-story farmhouse, I loved sleeping upstairs when it rained. It, too, was roofed with tin and resounded with the music of the rain. The rhythm was broken occasionally by the sudden sweep of rain from the branches of the big red elm trees as the wind swept through them. To me, there is no more secure and cozy feeling than to snuggle down in bed at night and hear the rain beating on a tin roof.

Today, I stand on the porch of our mobile home here on Phillip's Run Road in Summersville. The rain is beating a steady tattoo on the tin roof. In my yard, my petunias stand with drooping heads, water-weary and bedraggled.

Across from us, the farmer's cornfield is awash in a sea of water. The creek that borders our property is slowly spreading across the edge of our neighbor's yard, drowning her roses and creeping closer to her house.

Where the creek empties into Muddelty Creek, which is already out of its banks, the water covers the road from one side to the other. Only the big coal trucks and some of the braver pickups are fording the flood and coming through.

Criss and I are water-bound, unable to make it through to come home to Clay County. We are snug in our little trailer, while the rain makes music on the tin roof. We could pretend to be a ship in a storm, Indians in a teepee, or early settlers in the wilderness. Somehow, it's not as much fun as it used to be.

And the rain continues.

The Clay Herald
June 19, 1989

Midsummer days drone by like the humming of a bee, languid, sleepy days marked by misty mornings and hot, sunshiny days. Above the spotted Joe-Pye weed, the butterflies hover, anxious to draw all the sweetness of summer from its blossoms. Late summer flowers are making their appearance now; the jaunty Turk's cap lily is beginning to show its spectacular, spotted orange flowers along the swampy places and ditch lines. The plumey flowers of the tall meadow rue constantly invite bees and butterflies to partake of its honey. In the meadows the purple sneeze-weed, looking much like its cousin the black-eyed Susan, dots the landscape with its daisy-like blooms. Out in the fields, the nutmeg-scented St. Anthony's cross mingles its shiny pink flowers with the ripening blackberries and all nature seems to slow down to a summertime crawl.

These warm summer evenings take my mind back to childhood days and joys of long ago. There is a dirt road up Ovapa and there is a gang of barefoot children playing. The blackberries have been picked earlier in the day, handed over to our mothers and we are free in that hour or two between chores and bedtime. Supper has been over for some time, dishes washed, and water carried from the pump in zinc buckets for the night. A late evening hush falls over the hills, and the air is beginning to cool after the hot summer sun has gone down. The songbirds chirp sleepily, and a whippoorwill's lonely call echoes from a hillside.

We are playing hide-and-seek and I can hear Margaret Ann reciting from the sycamore tree where she has her head hidden in the crook of her arm. "Bushel of wheat and a bushel of rye, who's not ready, holler I!" We are as quiet as church mice, hiding behind the tall stock tanks, Bud Coon's garage and the pump station. Then comes the call, "Bushel of wheat and a bushel of clover, who's not ready, can't hide over——I'm coming!"

Then the hunt was on. The game breaks up when Jeuell Beth and Janice Carole have to go home, as their hour is up. We gravitate to the Virginia office porch and launch into our favorite game of "Old Witch." It is a fancified version of "Base," but adapted to the three-sided porch that runs the length and front of the office and tool house. As the oldest girl, I usually have to be the old witch and Cody tolls me away from the big metal tool chest that is my base. Alen Wayne rescues Larry from my clutches, while Mary Ellen sneaks around the back.

We have already exhausted "Pretty Girl Station" with its singsong chant, "Here I come . . .Where you from? . . Pretty girl station . . .What's your trade? . . . Lemonade . . . What's your initials? . . Get to work and show us something!"

Summer memories like sun—dappled shadows come and go, full of children from the past. I can hear Opal calling for Reva to come home and Mary has called Margaret Ann for the second time. Alen Wayne's house is adjacent to the Virginia office and we see Maxine stepping out on the porch to call him in. We know that it is just a matter of minutes until Mom is calling us to come in and get ready for night time devotions and Cody is already on his way home.

Long ago children—where are they now? They are scattered here and there and some of them, like Cody and Alen Wayne, are gone forever from this life. Yet in these long summer evenings, they romp and play in the meadows of my mind, young and happy once again. I can hear Mom calling, "Alyce Faye, Larry, Mary Ellen, Mark—it's time to come home!"

The Clay Herald
August 7, 1989

CHAPTER 5

HARVEST TIME AND PARTY TIME

A haze on the far horizon,
The infinite, tender sky,
The ripe, rich tint of the
cornfields,
And the wild geese sailing
high—
And all over upland and
lowland
The charm of the goldenrod,
Some of us call it Autumn,
And others call it God.

...William Herbert Carruth

It was summer one day and autumn the next. The sultry, scorching weather was swept away by the soothing rain that fell all night and most of the next day. There is change in the air, as the cry of the katydids grows slower and slower in the cooler nights.

The songbirds are restless as they, too, feel the urgency of the changing season. Whippoorwills swooped and circled aimlessly overhead yesterday evening, much like a crowd of anxious young matrons sorting out their respective youngsters after a day at the park.

We sit on the porch swing and listen to the night sounds as the fall insects fervently sing their farewell to summer. Darkness falls on Pilot Knob and the cool night air is pleasant as we swing and talk over the day's events. Silent are the frogs' high-pitched voices that spiced our springtime evenings; gone also are the twinkling lights of the lightning bugs that dotted the warm summertime air. Only the melancholy creaking of the crickets and katydids is heard as we sit in the gathering darkness.

It brings back memories of long-ago evenings when we would sit on the porch when the day's work was done. The front porch was always one of the most pleasant places to sit on the farm. Warm summer evenings would find us gathered there; sitting together in warm companionship on the swing or sprawled out on the rough boards of the porch itself.

Milking would be done; the milk strained and poured in the white enamel pans in the refrigerator. Daddy would be tired from working in the garden in the searing sunshine and be ready to rest awhile before we gathered back in the big front room for our nightly Bible reading and prayer.

Mom was constantly busy; even after we girls took over the dishwashing chores, she would always be sewing or mending until bedtime. The dishes would be washed, dried and put away and the big aluminum dishpans hung on their nails on the kitchen wall behind the cookstove.

The boys would carry in the water for the night in zinc buckets and set it on the water table with the tin dipper plunged into one of them.

The chores would all be finished and even Mom could be persuaded to sit down for a few minutes and enjoy the evening. We would listen to the hauntingly sweet notes of the whippoorwills as they called from hillside to hillside.

Many seasons have come and gone and many whippoorwills have sounded their liquid notes since then. But sitting on the porch in the twilight is a pleasure that has never faded.

The front porch was an indispensable part of our life. It was not only a place to rest and communicate with one another until nightfall it was a good place to visit with neighbors. People lived more leisurely back then and when someone passed the house, they could usually be persuaded to "come in and set a spell." If the swing was crowded, a straight-back kitchen chair or two would be dragged out for visiting neighbors.

Woodbine grew thickly on the rough porch posts and shaded the eyes from the hot summer sun. On one end, red and pink rambler roses twined their thick vines and bloomed the summer long. It was a most pleasant place.

The porch swing was an ideal place to court. In fact, it was the only place permitted, other than the living room. With six younger brothers and sisters, the porch swing was a more private place for me. We would sit on the swing on peaceful, warm evenings and hear low, murmured conversation from Mom's and Daddy's open bedroom window. We would smell the spicy odor of the cinnamon "tater" vine that grew up the porch post, and life was young.

Front porch sitting seems to have become a thing of the past. The newer homes are built without the graciousness of the open front porch;

instead decks and patios are built in the privacy of the rear of the house.

No longer does the front porch seem to beckon to the passing neighbor to stroll by and visit or does the family gather there to watch the passing parade. Folks seem too busy to sit down and visit for a while. Even in the family unit, members seem to be going their separate ways, never taking time to simply sit and talk to one another and enjoy the cool of the evening.

We need the front porch; we need the front porch swing, and we need to take time to sit down and rest a spell. It is still the place to relax and enjoy soft summer evenings.

Sometimes we sit in wordless communication and let the soothing motion of the porch swing lull our cares away. Porch sitting will bring a family closer together and make memories that will last a lifetime.

I hope I never get too busy to sit on the porch swing.

The Clay Herald
September 16, 1991

The Charleston Gazette
September 20, 1991

A fat harvest moon, like a round orange pumpkin, hangs suspended in the clear nighttime sky, illuminating the landscape with white brilliance. The world is bathed in silvery light, while black shadows lurk beneath each bush and tree. The only sounds heard are the papery rustle of dry cornstalks and the mournful cry of a few crickets.

The words of a song of my youth comes forcibly to mind: "Don't let the stars get in your eyes, don't let the moon break your heart. Love blooms at night, in daylight it dies, don't let the stars get in your eyes . . ."

The young girl who is trapped in this middle-aged body hears the call of the moon and she wants to be released to sing and run and play again. Those long-ago nights when the harvest moon shone full and bright was the signal for our "play parties" to begin.

The summer was a season of hard labor and every child that was big enough had to do his share. The days in the cornfield were hot and backbreaking, cutting the weeds and hoeing the corn over and over until it was laid by. Nighttime brought sore, aching muscles and tired bodies that fell exhausted into bed.

There was no leisure time during the growing season. The vegetable garden had to be weeded, hoed and fertilized. Deep summer brought blackberry season and gallons and gallons of blackberries to be picked and canned. Those who lived closer to the higher mountains also had huckleberries to pick, although they were scarce here in this area. Our parents had to scrape and save to make a living and anything that could be picked or harvested for the winter months was utilized.

Then there was the haying season. Those who have never worked in the hot hay field don't know the true meaning of labor. We had no modern equipment (of course, it was small scale, else we couldn't have coped) and the cutting and raking was done by a horse and human labor.

We would rake the cut hay in wind-rows, to be piled around a stack pole for tall haystacks. We filled the top of the barn full of loose hay, cramming it tight in the hayloft. We never baled it, but used a pitchfork to fill the mangers full for the cattle. Pitching the hay from the wagon into the loft was another strenuous job and it was muscle-straining work to pack it into each corner. Sometimes we worked frantically to get the hay in before a threatening thunderstorm hit and it was a great relief when every wisp was stored.

When the garden was all gathered in, down to the last orange pumpkin and green cushaw, and all that was left was the brown fodder shocks, we deserved to have some fun. Back then we had no built-in entertainment, so we made our own. We were not passive spectators watching someone else perform, but we were eager participants in our own games. It didn't take much to plan a party; just a moonlit night and a fall nip in the air.

The word soon got around (we had no telephones, either) that we were going to "gather up" at the Virginia office and have a party. Sometimes it was a "farewell party" for one of the neighborhood boys who was leaving for the armed forces and other times it was to simply get together. Someone would gather some dry branches and we'd soon have a nice bonfire going. There was no alcohol involved and the "drugs" were aspirin that we took for a headache. The benevolent harvest moon shining upon us, the sharp tang of the wood smoke hanging in the air and the crowd of young boys and girls generated enough excitement for all of us.

It is a shame that these old games are dying out. Daddy never allowed us to square dance, but looking back now those ring games that we played were almost the same thing. It was clean, innocent fun and young and old both participated in it. Some of the words and music are still fresh in my mind. Just this week, one of the games that I hadn't thought of in years came to me. Do you remember "Pig in the Parlor?" How we would swing and promenade when "we got a new pig in the parlor?"

What fun and excitement we had playing those games! Dressed in our broomstick skirts, kicking our heels that were clad in saddle oxfords and bobby socks, we would skip and twirl until we were breathless. Yes, we dressed up for these parties. Floating in on a cloud of Evening in Paris cologne (and some of the girls sported Blue Waltz) we felt irresistible.

Cheeks red with excitement, we skipped and sang to "Oh, the old dusty miller and he lived on a hill; He worked all day with a pretty good will. One hand in the hopper and the other in the sack, the ladies step forth and the gents turn back!" Remember how the line of boys turned in reverse, and we sang, "Here we go a-sowing oats, and who will be the binder? I've lost my true love, and right here I'll find her!"

After all these years, the tune still rings in my ears like yesterday. I wonder how old these games are and if some of them didn't come over with our forefathers from another country. Such as, "Here comes Miss Molly Brown, show me the way to London town." I must confess that I loved that one (it was a kissing game) and "Four in the Boat" holds a special place in my heart. It was at one of these fall parties that I met my future husband and he literally swung me off my feet playing that game. (The marriage has lasted 45 years now.)

I am happily content in my role as wife, mother and grandmother. I have no desire to go back and live my life over, as I have heard others express.

But on one of these fall-scented nights, with the leaves drifting to the ground and the orange harvest moon coming up over Pilot Knob—just one more time I'd like to be 16 again. I'd like to join hands with Betty Marie and Avis June, with Alen Wayne and Cody, with Peggy Ann and Donald Ray and exchange an innocent Juicy Fruit kiss and sing lustily, "There goes a bluebird through the window . . . old Virginia style!"

The Charleston Gazette
September 23, 1994

The Clay County Free Press
September 28, 1994

I hear Hickory Knob calling me. It comes clearly through these early October mornings, when the mist is rising from the hills and the sun is coming up on another perfect day.

Up there, the maple leaves are falling in a golden shower upon the forest floor, and the warm sunlight filters through the trees. I can close my eyes and smell once again that sweet, earthy fragrance that was unique to that place. No place on earth smells exactly like that to me.

It is the nutty smell of fall, composed of hot sunshine on rich soil, fallen leaves, and late fall flowers. It seems to rise from the creek bed, where the clean water carries the red, gold and brown leaves downstream in a slow, lazy movement. It is a magical, isolated spot where peace abounds. The piney odor of the hemlock and elusive perfume of the rhododendron add their fragrance to that clean air, creating a place that a person longs to go back to, and remembers always.

Daddy took us every fall to camp there during squirrel season. After we were married and had children of our own, we all had to go. Some years we camped on Ha'nted Lick and other times we would pitch our tent on Alfred's Fork. I remember one year when we camped on Alfred's Fork in a grove of maple trees and left our tent to come home for the weekend. When we returned, the maple trees had let loose their hoard of golden leaves and literally covered our tent, the table and the whole campsite in a covering of purest gold. We were rich indeed.

We looked forward each autumn to our return to nature, Daddy most of all. He always saved some of the pink-streaked yellow tomatoes to eat with squirrel gravy and biscuits that Mom baked in a Dutch oven in the campfire.

The first thing Daddy did after we got the camp set up was to cut us a grapevine swing. After we were mature women, his girls still swung on the grapevine. At night, we would build up a roaring fire and while we roasted marshmallows, Daddy would tell us scary stories of the Ha'nted Lick. His mother was raised in that part of the country and had experienced some of the strange happenings that had given that place its name.

As the campfire blazed and flickered, we would shiver at his tales of mysterious noises coming from the Lick itself; of cowbells ringing and people talking when there were no cows or people there. The shadowed woods at our backs seemed darker and full of danger and we would move closer to the fire and one another. Daddy's voice droned on and on and delicious shivers would travel up and down our spines. We felt safe only when we were securely zipped up in the tent at bedtime.

The last time we went with Daddy, we camped at Hickory Knob and the family had expanded to the place where there were several carloads of us. The woods resounded with the laughter and shouts of a multitude and any self-respecting squirrel would have left the country.

Daddy's hearing had gotten so bad that he couldn't hunt with the boys and Mom was afraid for him to go in the woods alone. His grandson, Noel, was just a little tyke, so he decided to go with Daddy. Daddy told us later that he and Noel were trudging up the hill and he told his young grandson, "Some day, Noel, you will be a big boy and come up here to camp and hunt. But your old Poppy won't be with you. I'll be gone but you can still carry on." Daddy said he heard a muffled sniffle, and turned around to see that Noel was crying. The words were truly prophetic. Daddy suffered a massive stroke the very next year that ended his camping and hunting days forever.

I have been up to Hickory Knob since and everything remains much the same. The big beech tree below Uncle Homer's, where we camped so often, has been cut down but the silver minnows still dart in the icy creek. The moss grows thick and green in the woodsy places, and the deer berries grow yet on the same huge rocks that line the creek.

The wild grapes hang from the treetops, dusky and blue, and the vines are ready to cut for a grapevine swing. The same sweet fragrance, full of fall and memories, is still there. So much the same, and yet so much is missing.

It is Daddy.

The Charleston Gazette
October 16, 1992

Summer has departed. When the blue moon in September came and white frost sparkled in the glow of it, she couldn't stay any longer. Swiftly and silently, she stole away in the night, leaving the Harvest Moon to shine on in solitary splendor. The tender summer flowers cried and wilted away as her departure left them in the icy clutches of the deadly frost and the few forlorn vegetables still in the garden were left blackened and bereft.

We cannot mourn her passing overlong, as October begins to flaunt her matchless autumn days. "The season of mists and mellow fruitfulness," (as Keats called it) comes with the golden days of October. I would like to hoard them, as a miser does his gold, counting each one out slowly and savoring all the fullness from dawn to dusk. These mellow autumn days, with early morning mist and hot sunshine later in the day, deep blue skies and glorious sunsets, changing leaves and late fall flowers, strike a responsive chord deep in my soul.

After summer's hurried pace, these slow, leisurely days are a blessing. There is time now to take a walk through the woods and fields and explore nature's ever-changing scene. It is impossible to return from even a short walk without having your arms laden with flowers. Purple ironweed, blue gentians, yellow goldenrod—weeds to some but beauty far surpassing any hothouse variety of flowers to those who love the hills. They begged to be picked and arranged in a bouquet to grace any table.

The colder weather is ripening the persimmons now, turning their puckery texture to a soft, mellow pulp. Daddy used to take all of us on a hike to Hick's Holler this time of year, and there was a persimmon tree that grew there, always dripping with sweet persimmons. All seven of us children trailed along after Mom and Daddy, snatching clusters of hazelnuts from the bushes and picking up the fallen hickory nuts.

The love of the woods and nature was ingrained in us from babyhood and Hick's Holler was one of our favorite places to explore. The memory of those long-ago days returns with October and are sweet and warm on my mind.

* * * * * * * *

The deep red of the oak trees have come into their own now, as most of the other trees have shed their leaves and lifted bare branches to the sky. Gaunt outcroppings of rock formations are clearly seen on the hillsides and are a stark contrast to the brown leaves that huddle at their base. The sheer rock cliffs that hang over the river bluffs have an austere beauty and are a symbol of the enduring quality of our hills.

Buzzard Rock was the "big" rock of my childhood. Situated on the ridge between Grannies Creek and Wallback, it is probably 50 or 60 feet high. It has been visited through the years by most local folk and is covered by names and initials carved on the rock.

When I was a little girl, the only access to it was a path that wound through the woods and to reach the summit a person had to climb straight up a crack in the sheer face of the rock. We wondered many times through our childhood about this particular rock, then Cousin Leo enlightened me about the history of it.

It seems that many years ago old people held church meetings on the top of it. There was a story back then that a "fat man" became wedged about halfway up the rock crevice one Sunday and prayed so loud that the preacher came back down and converted him right on the spot. They still had quite an ordeal prying him out of the crack in the rock.

Leo also related that there was a cave at one time on the Wallback side, with stone steps carved out leading down into the opening underneath the rock. My father had told us this story many times about this cave and how one of his boyhood friends (was it Dick Bullard?) had ventured for a distance down these steps, leaving an iron shucking peg to prove that he had gone that far. By the time we visited the spot, rubble had fallen in and covered the steps and obscured the cave opening.

We made up many fanciful tales of how the Indians must have used the cave many years ago and indeed an older civilization than that may have carved the steps. Leo said that he once dug in several places under the cliff and found some arrow points, an old stone axe and pieces of charred bones, which appeared to be deer bones. He also found two copper bracelets and a .36-caliber mountain rifle round lead bullet. Old timers say that Indians and hunters may have used the cave during cold and rainy weather.

Buzzard Rock is not the same as it was in my childhood. The oil company made a road up to the crest of the rock and the hair-raising climb up the face of it has been eliminated. It looks much smaller now and the mystery that surrounded it is gone. Now it is simply another rock, out in the middle of nowhere.

Daddy once took his Sunday school class of girls to Buzzard Rock on a picnic. I was along of course, with Jeuell Beth and Janice Carole Everson, Mabel and Betty Payne, Artha Lee Drake, Rosalie and Nina Faye Brown, Wanda and Wanitta Oxley, and probably others that I can't remember. We had an unforgettable day and one that can never be repeated.

* * * * * * * *

Cousin Leo was very familiar with Hick's Holler, too. He knew every rock and tree on this farm and Hick's Holler

151

was one of his haunts. He wrote me an interesting letter back in the spring about that place.

It seems that when he was a boy here on this farm, he was standing in the yard at midnight when a meteor or shooting star fragments hit the hillside across the creek. The sky lit up as bright as day and he found three of the still-warm fragments the next day. Another larger portion had landed in Hick's Holler, where he found the impact crater in an open field. It was wet that night, but the ground was scorched around the edges of the crater, which was six or seven feet across, and two or three feet deep. He took a fragment home and broke it open with a hammer and the inside looked like iron with a black, burned crust on the outside. A magnet would stick to it. He wrote, "If the Lord lets me live, someday I may be able to show the crater to you. I know just where it is, having rabbit hunted many times in that area."

He wrote in a previous letter about an unmarked grave on the farm here; old-timers said it was a little girl who passed away in the 20's (I know where the grave is; a spreading dogwood tree hovers over it, and weeds never grew there.) He made a map of the grave and said that he used to place flowers on the lonely, solitary grave when he was a little boy. He mentioned the fact that there are many unmarked

cemeteries across Clay County, graves
marked by two rough stones, as this
small grave was.

He will never show me the crater
made by the meteorite or the sad little
grave alone on the hillside. He lies in
his own resting-place here in the Clay
County hills that he loved.

The Charleston Gazette
October 8, 1993

The Clay County Free Press
October 19, 1993

The sun struggles vainly to break
through the overcast sky this morning
and the air is heavy with the threat of
impending rain. The honey-sweet scent
of the tiny, white wild asters hangs in
the air, mingled with the nutty
fragrance of dry, fallen leaves. The
bronze-gold beech trees across the
creek gleam dully on this cloudy day,
and the temperature slowly grows
cooler.

A bright green katydid humps up in
the flowerbed and looks forlornly at
me. I know he is cold but I also know
that he fiddled his summer away while
the honeybees buzzed frantically from
flower to flower to store their food
for the winter. He is shivering in the
cold while the industrious ant, after a

summer of hard work, is nestled underground surrounded by stores of food for the coming season.

There is something in the air that brings a sense of urgency to get ready for cold weather ahead. Neat piles of firewood, stacked and covered from the weather, give the assurance of a warm house on a cold, snowy day. The country housewife gets the same warm, secure feeling when she views the cellar shelves full of canned food and the potato bin overflowing with big, brown potatoes.

Folks nowadays don't prepare for winter the way we used to when I was a kid. Our entire summer was spent in raising a big garden, then canning, pickling and preserving every scrap of it. We scoured the fields for blackberries, which were canned in half-gallon jars and also made into jams and jellies.

Fifteen-gallon churns held the sauerkraut, pickled beans and ears of pickled corn. We buried our potatoes in a hole in the garden, nestled on a bed of hay and covered with more of the same. A tall hill of dirt was mounded over all and when we opened the potato hole, we would dig out the crisp, unwrinkled potatoes.

Apples were sometimes stored in the same manner and onions were pulled and hung by their tops in the barn loft.

When frost threatened, Daddy would pick off the green tomatoes, wrap them individually in squares of newspaper and store them in a cool place. We nearly always had ripe tomatoes for Thanksgiving, and sometimes even later.

We dug the fat white and yellow sweet potatoes (after first cutting off the vines to keep them from getting frostbitten, which made black streaks through the potato). These, too, were stored along with orange pumpkins and the winter squash.

Thanksgiving brought hog butchering time and our supply of meat for the winter. Sausage, ribs and backbones and sometimes the shoulders were canned, lard was rendered, and the hams and bacons were smoked.

The skin of the hog was rendered in the oven for additional lard and we used the crisp cracklings in corn bread and ate the crunchy pork rinds. The feet were scraped and pickled and the head was cooked in a huge pot and the meat picked off to make souse or head cheese. The ears were cooked and added to it.

My brother Mark was working one time on a construction job when one of the men pulled a sandwich out of his dinner bucket and slowly unwrapped it. Lifting the top slice of bread, he exposed a whole hog ear, white and glistening, on his sandwich. Mark gulped and put his lunch away.

We used almost everything about
the hog, except his grunt. We ate the
heart and liver but we didn't eat the
lungs.

One old-timer, who lived up on the
side of Pilot Knob many years ago, had
a sick spell right after hog-killing
time. His wife told my dad that Bill
had eaten a "whole set of hog lights."

Mom did use all the extra scraps
of fat to make homemade soap. We used
it for laundry, scrubbing and general
cleaning. She still makes an occasional
batch and it is in great demand by the
family.

It is no longer a struggle to make
it through a hard winter until spring
comes and the first wild greens appear.
Folks make a weekly foray to the
supermarket and fill their shopping
carts with cans of vegetables, bags of
potatoes, packaged meats and ready-to-
eat products.

It is much easier, without all the
hard labor and mess. But I sometimes
wonder what people would do if they had
once again to fall back on their own
resources.

The Charleston Gazette
October 22, 1993

CHAPTER 6

THE SPLENDOR OF SPRING

> *"She comes with gusts of*
> *laughter,—*
> *The music as of rills;*
> *With tenderness and*
> *sweetness,*
> *The wisdom of the hills."*
> *...Bliss Carman*

I heard Spring singing this morning.

It was barely breaking day; night shadows lay yet on the hilltops as Dawn peeped shyly through fingers of pink. Waterlogged ground had frozen in the night and dead spears of brown grass were frosted and stiff. The bare branches of the trees shivered in the early morning cold, supplicating naked arms reaching forward. The massive icicles that marched so proudly across the face of the rock cliffs had frozen in the very act of thawing and lay welded together in awkward, dispirited heaps on the ground.

Everywhere was the brown of winter. Brown leaves turned to browner earth, outmoded garments discarded carelessly by trees anxious to go to bed last fall. Broomsage patches gleamed with their golden-brown heads held aloft while the once-red berries of the sumac were now a dull brown. Garden patches were desolate and empty save for the cut-off corn stalks stubbornly testifying to last year's crop of corn. Dried, brown weed stalks lined the creek, although the raspberry canes shone with a whitish frost on its purple-brown arms.

It was hard to see Spring in the midst of all this brownness. But there she was, perched on the highest limb of the tall sycamore tree standing at the edge of the yard. A minuscule fluff of feathers about the color of one of the brown sycamore balls hanging from the tree and not much bigger, her song floated out on the clear morning air.

And what a mighty song came from that wee-feathered throat—a song of such longing and hope and good cheer that the heart of each listener was lifted. Across the slumbering hills and winter-weary land it drifted, telling of wonders to come.

She told of rich soil being tilled in the springtime—long, dark strips of earth curling up behind the keen edge of the plow. And of the grubs and earthworms uncovered in the sunshine, awaiting the sharp, yellow bills of her kinfolk. She revealed secret places hidden from curious eyes—tiny nooks and crannies where intricate, woven nests could be built. She sang of the grape arbor, where among the twisted vines a home would be made for helpless, naked birdlings. And how first the miniature eggs are laid—one at first and then another and another until Mother Nature says there are enough. Each tiny egg contains life and beauty and a world of song.

In her liquid notes, she told of the tender, new grass that would grow under the grape arbor—not the tough, wiry grass trampled underfoot but grass soft as velvet. How every year, purple violets push their way through to spangle the yard with gems of amethyst.

She sang with longing of how her maternal heart beat with joy when the eggs pulsed with life and the baby birds began to peck their way out of the confining shell. She grew joyous as she described the mother love that filled her heart as the helpless babies opened their mouths and cried for nourishment—and how she worked and slaved in an endless cycle to satisfy their voracious appetites.

She described how the grape leaves grew full and sheltered the home from rainstorms that sometimes blew violently and from the sun's heat that waxed hotter. She told of the satisfaction of seeing her young grow strong enough to try their wings and leave the nest, freeing her to repeat the same life-giving cycle once more. The musical warbling went on and on, revealing how anxious she was to start.

Winter is not over. The North wind will blow, snow will likely fall on the hills and ridges and icicles can form once again on the rock cliffs. But I have hope.

I heard Spring singing this morning.

The Clay Herald
February 25, 1991

February has turned over her crocuses, budding Easter flowers and passing snow flurries to capricious

160

March and flown away on the wings of a strong southwest wind. March seems to have come in like a vigorous lamb, but could be showing a few lion-like teeth before the day is over.

I love the March wind. How we welcomed it as kids, when it meant the mud would be drying up and we could dig out our carefully hoarded marbles and begin the springtime games. The earliest sign of spring, after the spring peepers began their musical chorus, was the tight circle of boys ringed around a serious marble game. We girls played marbles too but far be it from us to join the boys. They would have withdrawn in scorn and anyway we played the "sissy" games of "Four Holes and a Peewee," while they played "Keeps." Technically, my brothers were forbidden to play for Keeps as it was considered gambling, yet they always had their pockets full of ill-gotten gains.

It was hard on the knees of our overalls. By the time spring rolled around, they were getting pretty thin around the edges and the knees were the first to go. Our mothers would patch the knees and the marble games would go on. It has been many years since I've seen a group of little boys playing marbles—I guess it has gone the way of rolling a hoop, (and we also rolled old automobile tires), and hop-scotch. About the only game of my childhood that I see my grandchildren play is

Monopoly. I don't think it will ever die.

March wind would dry up the mud puddles in our dirt road and our feet and bicycles would pack it hard as concrete. So many things hinged on "when the mud dries up" that we could hardly wait. We could quit wearing the galoshes and five-buckle "arctics" worn by our brothers. We could get the bicycles and wheeled toys out of the shed. It meant putting away the sleds and heavy winter coats and wearing lighter jackets and sweaters.

It would find Daddy cleaning out the barn and hauling manure to spread on the garden and Mom making an early lettuce bed. "When the mud dried up," the wild greens would pop through the drying soil, tender and tasty. The peppery "creasy" greens were the first to be harvested at our house and they are still a favorite of mine. Mom picks them yet in the spring before the garden is plowed and it is a treat to come in her kitchen and find cooked creasy greens and a pone of corn bread. To me, that still spells home.

We used to rake the dead weeds and debris from the garden "when the mud dried up," and pile the dried cornstalks and last year's refuse together to burn. This was called "burning off the garden." The idea was to burn the pests and insects along with the clearing of the garden patch. Now the flat-top mower used in the fall makes this task unnecessary. The weeds and mulch are already chopped up and ready to be plowed under. But I miss the burning smell of spring.

March is that lull between winter and spring; a needed interval while the earth gets her bearings before launching into full-fledged growing. I wonder if we humans don't need a period of dormancy to get our perspectives in order before the rush of the season is upon us. We get a chance to rake up some old prejudices, cut down ugly attitudes, and pile them together with bad thoughts and actions—then strike a match to the whole mess and watch them go up in smoke.

March, with all her shifting moods, is a prelude to spring and welcome in the hills. We can tolerate her sudden frantic snowstorms, knowing that the sun can be beaming down before the last snowflake hits the ground. And "when the mud dries up," there are so many things we can do. I think I'll hunt up some marbles and see if I can teach the grandsons how to play. Let's see, you dig four holes in a rectangle . . .

The Clay Herald
March 4, 1991

The Charleston Gazette
March 19, 1991

The swift waters of William's River have never lost their charm. Icy cold and sparkling, just as it was in my childhood, it swirls and ripples around huge rocks and massive fallen trees to form white caps and then flows on. The air is pure and clean, scented with pine needles and wood smoke. It is pure pleasure every spring to get away from the daily routine of life and camp out in the mountains.

Spring is a little late in coming here but there are unmistakable signs nevertheless. The mottled leaves of the dogtooth violet are peeping through the dry leaves, although the bloom has not yet appeared. Along the banks of the tributary where we made our camp, there are masses of spring beauties and wild anemone. On the forest floor, the bright yellow violet is appearing.

It was a delightful week. Although the weather was wet and rainy at times, the temperature was warm and part of our cooking was done outside over a campfire. One day Criss and I dug ramps, tender little ones that we almost had to dig out from under the leaves. We cooked them outside that evening, in an iron skillet with smoky bacon. When they had simmered a few minutes, we dumped in a bowl of beaten eggs. We fried potatoes over an open fire, along with a large skillet of fresh trout that was caught that day.

Thanks to the oven in Mike's camper, we had hot biscuits to round out the meal. It was a memorable feast and all agreed that the ramps were the most delicious item on the menu.

One year Daddy took a whole gang of us to William's River to camp and pitched a big tent for all of us to sleep. There were so many of us and we were crowded "pig and tail" inside the tent, that when one person wanted to turn over, he had to yell, "Turn!" Then everyone had to turn at the same time.

We gathered two bushels of ramps that day and must have eaten about half of them for supper. We all ate ramps except baby sister Susie. Bedtime came and we were jammed in the tent like sardines, all breathing ramps, except Susie. "Don't laugh!" she begged us. When we laughed, she yelled, "Laugh in some other direction!" I don't know how she survived the night but to this day she dislikes ramps.

My boys believe in breaking their children young to the joys of outdoor living. Kevin and Andy took Josh and Benji to Summit Lake while we were there and both of the five-year-olds caught a fish. The three-year-old youngsters, Jessica and Abigail, loved it. They toasted marshmallows over the fire, fell in the icy water a few times, and ran like wild Indians through the woods. Mike and Peggy joined us with their three little ones. Chrissie looks like a little lady with her curls and feminine ways but she can climb a tree with the best of them.

The next day was warmer, and even more beautiful. One day of sunshine had coaxed the wild flowers through the rich, black loam of the mountain soil and a variety of trilliums came in bloom. There were the large purple ones, looking regal and aloof above the more modest pink spring beauties. Pure white ones, called the large-flowered trillium, gleamed chastely among the dry, brown leaves covering the forest floor. Smaller red trilliums, also called toadshade, were scattered all around. Near a shady rhododendron grove bordering the river, I discovered a beautiful painted trillium, which is a white flower with a splash of pink in the center.

There was not a single cloud to mar the vast blueness of the sky. The air was clean and refreshing and the swift, swirling current of the water had a soothing effect. Sitting on one of the gigantic boulders that borders the river and hearing only the roar of the water as it surges around the immense rocks brings a peace to the soul that is needed in today's fast-moving world.

We have had many wonderful camping trips in this area. I remember a trip that Daddy made one time with my brother Mark and two of my sons, Kevin and Andy, when they were teenagers. They decided to really rough it and walk to the head of Tea Creek, which is at least six miles. They planned to eat what they caught and they strapped on an iron skillet (Daddy), two tomatoes (Kevin) and half a can of coffee (Mark).

It is wild, rough going up that creek, climbing over huge boulders, fallen trees and slippery spots. They still remember what a feast it was— fresh trout (native brown brookies) fried over an open fire, sliced tomatoes, (one was slightly mashed when Kevin sat down on it) and coffee strong enough to float a saw log.

It seemed that they had failed to include a coffeepot, so they had to brew it right in the coffee can. It was a waste not to use all the coffee, so they brewed half a can of coffee and half a can of water. After this stout meal they started back down the stream, tired but happy. The place seemed wilder, the boulders bigger and they began talking about rattlesnakes.

Daddy had to favor his back, because he had once fractured a vertebrae and also had a disc removed. Just as they were crawling down a slanting rock, Mark in front and Daddy inching his way behind Kevin, a wicked notion struck Mark. When he reached the bottom, he sneaked a plastic box of swivels out of his pocket and shook them.

He shrieked, "Rattlesnake!" and Kevin turned and climbed up Daddy and

knocked him flat on his back on top of
the iron skillet. He lay there, moaning
and groaning, and exclaimed, "Boys,
you've broke my back, and I don't know
how you are going to carry me out of
here!" After the excitement died down,
he realized that his back wasn't broken
but he did have a skillet-shaped circle
on his back.

These trips do promote
togetherness and bonds the family unit
tighter. If ours gets any tighter we'll
be welded together.

The Clay County Free Press
April 13, 1983

The Charleston Gazette
May 1, 1992

The great and mighty Heavenly
Father has opened the windows of heaven
and poured the blessing of springtime
upon our hills and valleys—almost too
much to contain. Pure, unadulterated
praise pours from a multitude of
feathered throats as the songbirds lift
their heads heavenward each break of
morn. A green haze hovers over the
hilltops as the new buds burst forth on
the trees and underfoot, the wild
flowers bloom in profusion. These tiny
harbingers of spring bloom shyly,
almost unnoticed, unless a person takes
time to stop and notice their beauty.

Blue violets are thickly carpeted in low-lying clumps and in the woods can be found the paler blue variety and also the downy yellow violet. Masses of bluets are found everywhere and the aptly named spring beauty shows her pink head. Golden ragwort adds a sunny note to the creek banks and marshy places and the lowly dandelion is a thing of beauty. There is a favorite place that I love to visit in the spring and I'd like to show it to you.

We have to take this old dirt road, it has been here as long as I can remember, and walk up the holler to where the road forks. It is such a pleasant day for a walk; the warm sun beams down and has touched all, the world with new life. On the hill, the sarvis berry blooms white and the dogwood puts out its blossoms of white, each petal tipped with brown. The redbud is in bloom now, masses of purple that contrast dramatically with the dogwood's white.

We leave the dirt road now and cross the creek to take a path across the meadow. The path is springy and soft beneath our feet with moss and grasses and the miniature yellow flowers of the cinquefoil twinkle by the wayside. The warming rays of the sun rest upon the scrubby pines that crouch on the gently sloping hillside and the air is scented with a fresh, piney smell. We breathe deeply of the good clean air and think how wonderful it is to be alive and healthy and able to enjoy God's creation.

Here we have to stoop down and crawl under the old barbwire fence and our path parallels the tiny creek that cuts its way down the mountain. We are out of sight and hearing of civilization and the stillness settles down like a blessing. The path meanders along the creek and the trees overhead blot out the sunshine.

The path widens and a moss-covered, fallen log gently invites one to stop and rest awhile. As we sit quietly on the log, the peace and tranquillity of the place begins to seep into our souls. The only sound is the rustle of a chipmunk in the dry leaves and the singing of a bird on a nearby bough. A rich, growing smell rises up from the black soil and everywhere there are spring flowers.

Clumps of wild anemones quiver in the light breeze, ranging in color from pure white to pale pink and blue. Wild geraniums, with their delicate, purple blossoms, grow in clusters along the creek and blue sweet Williams give out their heavenly scent. In this woodsy glade, the wild iris, looking so much like tiny orchids, bloom in blue splendor.

This is a place to rest one's mind from the cares of the world. We look around at so much beauty and can only humbly say, "Thank you, Lord, for making such a world as ours. Thank you for giving us eyes to see, ears to hear, and a mind to know that Thou hast made all things well."

We leave this place refreshed in body and soul and knowing that even the memory of it will bring peaceful thoughts in days to come.

The Clay County Free Press
April 24, 1985

May gathers her full green skirts about her and prepares to leave our hills. This has been a lush, green May, with gardens almost a full month ahead of past springs. These tropical rains and warm temperatures have combined to produce an atmosphere that is most conducive to growing things. The strawberries have hit their peak and are going downhill, although a scattering of red, juicy ones can be found bedded down in the grass. Freezer jam reposes in our freezer, summer sunshine captured in a glass jar.

The first day of June dawns bright and beautiful—she enters our hills crowned with roses and laden with first fruits. After last night's rain, the world is clean and scrubbed and sparkling with sunshine. Even the air is washed clean, cool and refreshing. The songbirds are having a jubilee this morning and my heart joins in their jubilant chorus. They are nesting everywhere now. I leaned over the grape arbor to smell the grape bloom and was buzzed by an alarmed robin (Have you ever smelled anything as exquisite as grapes in bloom? The air, as it blows from the woods, is full of the scent of wild grape bloom). Above my head was a nest of robin eggs, blue as the sky above and tended by a faithful mother bird. Murmuring an apology, I backed away while she twittered on the limb above me.

I have one broody hen that finally took to her nest in earnest. She is patiently setting on a clutch of brown eggs, fiercely squawking at every intruder. The tom turkey has taken up with me, as he is terrified of the rooster. He also recognizes me as the hand that feeds him. Every time I set foot out of the house, I am followed by at least two dogs and a turkey. And so my life continues in these hills . . .

My mind goes back to childhood days, and Junes long past. We were glad in the freedom of "school let out," and it seemed that summer would go on forever. The biggest decision we had to make was where to play the next day. One of our favorite places was the "Big Rock" across the creek. Actually, it was part of the creek bed and during periods of rainy weather it would be completely covered with water. Most of the time, however, the creek flowed gently beside it and the woods on the other side crowded right down to the edge of the rock.

On the creek bank, there was a seam of grayish-blue clay mud that was ideal for mud pies and cakes and also for forming vases, cups and saucers. We would spend hours on end on that sun-baked rock, kneading the soft clay mud and liberally besmearing ourselves as well. In June, the rambler roses would be blooming and we would make elaborate wedding cakes lavishly decorated with red and pink roses. The clay mud bank, like my days of childhood, has disappeared now without a trace.

There was a cleft in the Big Rock that made a beautiful natural aquarium. We kept it well stocked with tadpoles, minnows, penniwinkles and crawdabs. We also caught lizards and salamanders but I drew the line at hellgrammites. I couldn't stand to pick up something that threatened to pinch me with the other end.

After each summer rainstorm, the creek would rise and wipe out our collection of marine life. It kept us busy keeping our aquarium stocked.

The creek seemed much bigger then, or perhaps it was because we were smaller. As the days grew hotter, we were drawn more and more to the cool recesses of the creek. We began early in the spring begging Mom to let us go wading. Finally, she would give us permission to wade only, with a strong admonition not to get wet all over.

Invariably, we fell down in the creek. Then after we were already wet, it was a shame not to take advantage of it. We usually spent two or three hours wallowing around in it before we went to the house to tell Mom that we had fallen down. It was amazing how four of us at one time managed to accidentally fall down but she didn't say too much. Maybe she was remembering when she was a little girl herself and she and her sisters would wade Big Laurel Creek to the tune of "Knee deep-knee deep!"

Yes, June was lightning bugs and hide-and-seek played in the gathering dusk. It was the piercing-sweet call of the whippoorwill and Mom's voice calling us in at bedtime. It was the carefree days of youth and never fully appreciated until they are gone.

The grandchildren have been busy as usual, brightening up our days. Six-year-old Josh planted one pinto bean beside his porch. It came up nicely and began to vine upward. He returned home from school one day to find that the wind and rain had blown his vine down on the ground. He thought it was ruined completely and was deeply mourning his loss. Kevin showed him that it was still growing; that it was only beaten down by the rain. "That's all right, Daddy," he said bravely. Then he added, "I don't know why I planted that thing anyway. I don't even like pinto beans!"

Patty's little one, Adrian, who is barely two, is following right in his brother Luke's footsteps. Patty was spraying her potato patch one day last week and Adrian was playing near her. My brother-in-law, Howard, had finished plowing and parked his tractor nearby. They heard the sound of the tractor running and looked up to see Adrian calmly driving the tractor through the garden. He had climbed up on the seat, turned the key on and began plowing.

Howard was rooted to the ground with shock but Patty kicked off her shoes and chased him down. He had to show her where the key was before she could turn it off. She said he did a pretty good job—plowed one swath through the garden and missed the tomatoes. Who said country life is dull?

The Clay County Free Press
June 5, 1985

Wonder why you never hear of stone bruises any more? These came as frequently as a summer thunderstorm and were one of the more painful aspects of growing up in the country. We suffered them periodically when I was a kid, excruciating infections deep in the heel or ball of one's foot. Only we didn't call them infections—we had "bealin's" on us. I can remember

Grandpa saying, "This young'en's got a bealin' on her foot."

It was probably a combination of too much jumping and not enough shoes. Shoes were worn to church in the summer (endured rather than worn). They were usually taken off as soon as we got out of sight of the church and slung across the shoulder.

We never walked when we could run. And jumping was one of our favorite recreations. A favorite game of ours was jumping out of the second story loft of the old log barn and we would spend hours climbing back up the ladder to the loft, in order to jump out the window once more. None of us would take a dare. All we had to say was, "I dare you—or I double-dare you," and we would try any hair-raising thing. The rest would follow suit, as no one wanted to be branded a coward.

Jumping was such fun then. There is something in the heart of almost every country kid that makes you feel that you can fly, under the right circumstances. Jumping off the Virginia office porch roof or the roof of the house, almost made you feel that you were really flying. In the woods, we would climb slender saplings to the top and bend them down, sometimes dropping the last eight or ten feet to the ground.

With all this, it is a wonder we didn't suffer broken arms, legs and heads. The only fracture we suffered was when little sister Jeannie fell off the yard gate and broke her arm. We did suffer stone bruises, though.

At the first sign of a stone bruise, Mom or Daddy would put a poultice on the affected area. This could be wilted plantain leaves, sassafras leaves pounded into a pulp or pine resin to draw out the infection. One of the best poultices that Mom made was catnip leaves, milk and meal cooked together and applied as hot as a kid could stand it. These were all tied on the foot with a clean white rag. We crippled around for a few days with the poultice, then Daddy would decide that it was time for surgery.

I can still feel that quiver of apprehension, as he would carefully sterilize a needle and a single-edged razor blade with alcohol and put us belly down on the couch.

It probably wasn't as painful as it seemed then. He would lift each layer of skin (our feet were as tough as shoe leather) with the needle and make paper-thin cuts with the razor blade, until he cut into the actual infection. Then came the fun. He would squeeze the opening until he got the "core" out, then apply alcohol and another poultice. In a couple of days, we would be well and jumping out of the barn again.

I remember one bealin' that didn't respond to home remedies. It came on the tip of my finger and in a few days was a throbbing, aching pain that extended down my whole arm. Mom tried all the home remedies that she could think of, even to tying a piece of fat pork on the end of my finger. One night in particular, I remember walking the floor in the dark (a sudden thunderstorm had caused a power outage) and crying. Mom had scraped a raw potato and used it for a poultice and it seemed to hurt worse.

She told Daddy, "I believe she has a bone felon," and the next day we made one of our infrequent trips to the doctor.

Doc Smith squinted at it and said, "It is a bone felon" (Maybe Mom couldn't cure it, but she could diagnose it). He proceeded to squirt some kind of liquid on it, then took a scalpel and with one quick slash opened it to the bone. It got well almost overnight, although a little sliver of bone came out with the infection.

These things didn't slow us up much, as we were back in the woods and barn as soon as we were healed. If you want to fly, you have to pay the price.

The Charleston Gazette
July 14, 1995

The Clay County Free Press
July 19, 1995

Hot and full-blown, summer comes breathlessly into the hills. She blows her sultry breath over the countryside, coaxing the gardens to grow and flourish and covers the hills with thick, green underbrush.

The early garden crops seem to grow overnight, while the weeds grow almost as fast as the vegetables. It is a continuous chore to keep the weeds and pests from overtaking the garden.

Gardening is such a rewarding task, though. There is something that satisfies the basic need in our hearts to provide food with our own hands. I love getting right down into the rich soil (no gloves for me) dropping the tiny seeds and setting out the tender plants.

Who could imagine that such a tall stalk of corn, with its full ears or the rambling bean vine covered with tender green beans could ever have come from just a little seed?

Cultivating the garden, pulling out the invading weeds and hoeing fresh soil up around the plants is a job that I enjoy. I didn't feel this way when I was a kid at home and working in the garden was one of our dreaded summertime chores. It is much easier now, with the garden tiller to work up the ground and make it easier to hoe.

Daddy used to hook up the work horse, Old Topsy, and run the plow through the garden, while we kids hoed behind him. There would be great clods of dirt that we would have to pound with the backs of our hoes and pulverize, so that we could hoe around the plant.

I don't know why, but the sweat bees used to be worse than they are now. We dreaded those pesky little bees that seemed to head for the bend of our elbows or the backs of our necks to loose their stinging darts. Once you mashed one, it seemed to drive the others into a fury and they would attack even more furiously.

Maybe everything seemed harder when you were a kid, but I got no joy out of gardening then. The sun seemed hotter, the rows longer, and it felt as if my whole summer was going to be spent in that endless garden.

Now, I enjoy my gardening tasks and take pride in the fruits of my labor. The bowls of crisp, new lettuce, dressed with hot vinegar and bacon grease, make the labor worthwhile.

We have had new potatoes out of son Andy's garden and all the lettuce and onions that we can eat. We had friends to visit from North Carolina last week and she inquired, when I brought in a bowl of freshly picked lettuce, "Are you going to kill that lettuce?" I have never gotten used to that expression but if you pour hot bacon grease and vinegar over it, it is bound to kill it.

I was thinking last week, while I worked in the garden, how easy it is to pull out the weeds while they are young and tender. The roots disengage easily and it is a simple task to pull them out between the plants. If they are not pulled out when they first appear, it takes a real effort to get the roots loose from the ground.

Then, too, if they are left until they grow to maturity, it is almost impossible to yank some of them out. Lamb's quarter and pigweed (amaranth) in particular are two weeds that put down such a root system that they resist even the most vigorous attempts to uproot them.

It is the same way with things that we allow to grow in our hearts. Wrong thoughts and attitudes, unresolved anger and grudges, are all weeds that we need to nip in the bud. They are easy to uproot if we pull them out as soon as we are aware of them. If allowed to grow, it becomes harder and harder to get them out of our minds and hearts. If unchecked, the roots will grow rampant until it is impossible to dig them out without God's help.

Wrong thoughts and attitudes grow into resentment and bitterness, while anger and grudges turns to unforgiveness and hatred. The root system will overgrow our hearts until we become embittered and miserable people, whose lives can only bear crops of malice and hatred.

No wonder the Bible warns us of letting any root of bitterness spring up and trouble you, because a person who allows these "wild weeds" to grow in his or her heart is the one directly affected by them. We can hold a grudge or unforgiveness in our hearts for someone who may not even be aware of it and the repressed anger in us can eat us alive.

These thoughts ran through my mind as I pulled up the little wild morning glories before they became entangled around the tomato and pepper plants and uprooted the tiny pigweed* and lamb's quarter greens.

I pray for good things to grow in my heart, such as more love, mercy and compassion for others, long-suffering and true forgiveness, which are the gifts of the Spirit and cultivated by Him.

The Charleston Gazette
June 23, 1995

The Clay County Free Press
June 28, 1995

Some people feel that springtime is not complete without a good mess of ramps. Ramps are a true mountain food, relished by many and scorned by some. I belong to the former group.

The dictionary tells us that they are a wild, onion-like plant found in eastern North America, with a characteristically strong odor; eaten by mountain folk during some of their spring festivals in the latter part of April. As the Queen of Sheba said to King Solomon, "The half was not told me." Ramps cannot be adequately described; they must be experienced.

They are an innocent appearing little plant with flat, broad leaves and a tender, white root. Ramp addicts have been known to dig under the leaves and unearth these delicacies before the leaf bud emerges from the ground. We had some of those this spring too.

As for eating them at festivals, I suppose a person could call ramp eating a festival at any time. My husband and I have enjoyed them as a cozy twosome, the piece de resistance of a romantic, candlelit table (This was in a camper where the only source of light was a candle stuck in a soda pop bottle). And it is a festive occasion when we get together as a family on our camping and fishing trips and cook ramps for everyone over an open campfire. As you drive along the road paralleling William's River, the aromas from the campfires mingle together into one great odorous homage to the lowly ramp. There is another particular feature of this wild plant—when you feast upon these seasonal victuals; you cannot smell the odor of them on anyone else. That is why we like to indulge when we are out in open country. Fortunately, everyone in our large family likes this food.

When my father was living, he liked to include everyone, from bald-headed infant to Grandpa on a cane, on his frequent camping trips. He had an enormous tent and we would still be packed in at night like sardines in a tin can. Mom would pin the quilts together with big safety pins (talk about togetherness) and if one fellow had to turn over, we all had to turn. The worst place to sleep was on the sides next to the wall of the tent, as the nights were often cold and sometimes the covers didn't stretch that far. It was rough also if you were positioned beneath the gaping safety pins.

We always dug a gunnysack or two of ramps for our own family festival. Mom kept a gigantic steel skillet for camping trips that held about a peck of ramps at a time and we put it to good use. We would sit down to a meal of fresh trout, potatoes fried over an open campfire, hot biscuits baked in a Dutch oven buried in the glowing coals and the ramps cooked with bacon and eggs.

We could hear the muted roar of the river in the background, as it rushed around boulders and fallen logs. The smoke of the campfire mingled with the aroma of warm pine needles and life was good indeed.

I wonder if ramps are an acquired taste, or do you fall in love with them at the first bite? I have been eating them for so long that I can't remember. When you grow up with them in your Pablum, it is hard to pinpoint that first taste.

A friend from Michigan told us that they grow there in his native state, but they call them wild leeks. He recalls that when he was a boy and got tired of going to school every day, all he would have to do was eat a few raw ramps and he would be invited to stay home for a few days. Raw ramps are actually the culprit when it comes to breath that you can slice with a knife. Cooked ramps don't linger on the breath all that long. A couple of days, maybe.

Ramps can be used in a variety of recipes—almost anything that calls for onions or garlic. I like them best simmered tender-crisp with some bacon and then add beaten eggs to the skillet.

They will rejuvenate your system, if they don't boost your popularity. The best way is to eat them with a gang of fellow ramp lovers, and pass the Sen-Sen.

The Charleston Gazette
April 24, 1992

Warm June sunshine beams down upon hills that are ready for summer, after the colder than usual springtime temperatures. The pale yellow and white blossoms of the viney honeysuckle covers road-bank and hillside alike with unforgettable fragrance. Fields of common daisies stretch in every direction and the newly mown lawn exudes the scent of sweet clover and crushed peppermint. A curtain of blue sky overshadows Pilot Knob and there is a feeling of peace and serenity in the atmosphere.

Daisies have always been a symbol of freedom to me. They appeared at the ending of the school term and heralded the beginning of summer. I guess there is no better feeling to a child than to know that school is out and summer vacation is at hand.

It wasn't that I didn't like school—I did. But after the weather grew warmer in the spring and the days ground out, dull and droning, it became a hardship to put in those last few weeks. No wonder the boys threw their caps in the air and shouted all the way down the hill on the last day! Summer loomed before us; days of fishing, playing in the woods, riding our bicycles and sleeping a little later in the morning.

It seemed that our parents saw summer in another light, though. While we were anticipating playtime, they were thinking of all the free labor that we represented—baby sitting (I always had a little one or two tagging after me, and sometimes a baby on my hip. I remember how insulted I was at one time when the boy next door, Alen Wayne, called me "the old woman that lived in a shoe." Now, I wouldn't trade the memory of those days of caring for those little ones for anything).

We were delegated to pick blackberries, work in the garden, fix fences (the boys) and get up early. You can believe that we were never bored. I remember when Crystal was still home and complained to me, "Mom, I am so bored!" When I informed her that she could clean her room and relieve that boredom, she recovered and said quickly, "I'm not that bored!"

While some of the farm chores were hard and tiresome, there were others that I enjoyed. Going after the cows for the evening milking was one of my favorite jobs. I don't know why the placid animals didn't have enough sense to come to the gap when milking time came but one of us kids would always have to climb the hill to the pasture field and herd the cows home.

The path wound uphill through the woods, steep and rocky. The moss was soft underfoot however and we were always barefoot in the summertime. Green leaves formed a canopy overhead and it was cool and shady. Sometimes it took quite a while to get to the upper pasture.

There were so many things to explore along the way. Silky, sweet ferns begged to be stroked and sniffed and the shiny green, heart-shaped leaves of wild ginger grew there. Pungent to the nose and bitter to the taste, I couldn't resist tearing off a leaf to chew. Then there was the speckled sweet birch bark to strip and enjoy and clusters of mountain tea would offer their tasty pink berries.

A person had to stop at the spring where the water gurgled like magic from under a rock, to get a drink and rest awhile. Sometimes an orange spotted salamander would crawl out from under a cool rock and contemplate the human person sitting there while it was being studied in turn.

Eventually, I would get to the upper pasture field, above the line of trees that marked the woods below. After a leisurely search for wild strawberries and admiring the wild flowers that grew in abundance, I would remember what I came for. The cows were always found in the far corner of the fence, still munching grass as if they had all the time in the world... We had a lot in common, those milk cows and I—we never got in a hurry.

After a gentle prod with a stick, they would start their ambling journey back to the gap. They would stop and graze awhile and I would study nature and pick a bouquet of wildflowers to take home. A ring of fairy mushrooms would catch my eye and I would spend minutes daydreaming about the elusive, magical creatures who gathered there and danced in the moonlight.

A striped chipmunk would dart into a hole nearby and this called for some intensive investigation. Belatedly, I would realize that the cows had stopped again and I would hurry them down the hillside.

Mom always wondered why it took me so long to go after the cows. It wasn't just a trip to bring in the cows—it was a lovely journey through a June day.

The Charleston Gazette
June 11, 1993

Another June, another high school graduation. After four times, you'd think we would be prepared. But somehow, each time one of ours dons the cap and gown and marches through the auditorium, there is that same familiar lump in our throats and the threat of tears dangerously near the surface. All at once, the knowledge is thrust abruptly upon us that these young people are no longer children but adults in their own right.

I cannot account for the years that have gone by so swiftly. Here is Matthew, our youngest son, ready to receive his diploma. Such a short time ago, he was a baby in my arms—now he is a tall, self-assured young man with an easy smile, standing in size-twelve shoes. I keep remembering how small he looked when he started to kindergarten. Our daughter Patty, who helped mother both of our younger children, shared a pang with me as he boarded the school bus and began an adventure that ends with his diploma this night. He looked back then, his blue eyes anxious beneath his fringe of blonde bangs and both Patty and I felt an urge to snatch him back in the house.

The years have gone by faster than a weaver's shuttle. His bedroom is a mixture of childhood and emerging adulthood—ranging from "Old Smoky," his teddy bear from babyhood days, to the grown-up prom pictures of him and Tammy. An old Monopoly set (oh, the hours he and Crystal spent playing that game!) shares the closet shelf with a padlocked box of love letters (from Tammy). Other outgrown childhood toys, untouched for years, are stacked in place—a race track, a chemistry set, an outfit to perform real magic tricks—all waiting for a child that will never return.

Under his bed is the electric guitar that he was so determined to learn to play, replaced by the stereo that is turned on as soon as he enters the room. These are bits and pieces of growing up that are soon to be discarded like an outgrown cocoon.

My heart hurts as I see him walk across the stage, putting childhood days behind him and beginning to accept adult responsibilities. I get the same feeling I had when he started to kindergarten—I want to snatch him back and protect him. I know that there are hurts and disappointments down the road for him, but he has to walk it on his own. There will be falls and bruises and scraped knees, but I won't be there to pick him up and patch the hurts. How we wish we could shield our children from life's harsh realities, but we cannot. Our children have to learn just as we did.

Right now it seems that we haven't prepared him for anything. The years we have spent trying to teach, to instruct to mold—have they been in vain? As I look at you now, Matthew, your wings still a little wrinkled and wet from your cocoon, I can't keep from wondering what lies ahead for you. You will have to learn to make your own decisions, even when they are wrong; I will have to learn to keep quiet, even when I know they are wrong.

If I could have one wish for you, Matthew, it would be for you to be happy. If we have taught you anything, I hope you have learned this: the highest state of happiness can be achieved only by obedience to God's laws. I know that life beckons with both hands and it looks so alluring and exciting. The popular thinking today is to live any way that you please; that nothing is really wrong anymore. Still, sin is sin and there is a reaping that cannot be avoided. Sin has a long range of consequences, which is always evil, always against us and we will always pay.

God loves you and wants you to be happy. We have tried to instill into you God's commandments from the time you were just a little boy. His commandments are holy, just and fair and are for our good and happiness. The moral evils of our day and time will lead to your destruction. They have the potential of bringing total destruction, not only to you as an individual but also to our culture and nation.

Oh, yes, Matthew, we would protect you if we could. But only God can lead you now and He can lead only as you yield yourself to Him. As I look at the fresh-faced young women and strong young men in this graduating class, I wish I could tell all of them this—find God, and find happiness.

The pattern for a happy life can be found in the pages of the Bible. Proverbs 3:1-4 says, "My son, forget not my law: but let thine heart keep my commandments: For length of days, and long life, and peace, shall they add

unto thee. Let not mercy and truth
forsake thee; bind them about thy neck:
write them on the table of thine heart:
so shalt thou find favor and good
understanding in the sight of God and
man."

                   THE BIBLE
We search the world for truth, We cull
The good, the true, the beautiful,
From graven stone and written scroll,
And all old weary flower-fields of the
soul;
And weary seekers of the best
We come back laden from our quest,
To find that all the sages said
Is in the Book our mothers read.

          ...John Greenleaf Whittier

               The Clay County Free Press
               May 29, 1985

               The Charleston Gazette
               June 12, 1992

CHAPTER SEVEN

OLD DAYS AND OLD WAYS

"Tell me the tales that to me were so dear,
Long, long ago, long, long ago."
...Thomas Haynes Bayley

The one- and two-room grade schools are a relic of the past. When I was a youngster, nearly every child attended one of these.

Hagar Grade School was a two-room school much like many others scattered about our state at that time. When the last few weeks of the school term began to drag by and the days grew hot and long, our "big room" teacher, Mr. Hinkle, would plan a field trip and take his entire room on a hike to the top of Pilot Knob. It was a nature study, an exercise program and a day of companionship all combined.

It is only in looking back that I realize what an excellent teacher Mr. Hinkle was. A big, red-cheeked man of German descent, he hid a soft heart beneath a gruff exterior. Over and over he drilled in us the value of a good education. In teaching four grade levels and covering every subject, he had to be knowledgeable in every area.

Arithmetic (not math) was the bane of my existence and each class had to go to the blackboard to work out their problems. I would struggle with the concept of math to no avail. His highest praise was, "You've got a head on you like a house cat!" Unfortunately, I didn't hear that applied to myself very often; it was more likely to be, "Maybe you should go soak your head in some stump water!"

He had great respect for a love of reading, however, and stocked our little bookcase with a variety of good books. Many times he refused to disturb me when I was engrossed in a book and oblivious to the fact that the rest of the class had gone to the blackboard to do their lessons. He introduced us to Jesse Stuart's books on the Kentucky hill country (very much like our own) and Zane Grey's novels of the Old West.

One of his passions was music. He loved to sing and actually taught his room to sing in four-part harmony. We used a Stamps-Baxter songbook and would belt out hymns with soprano, alto, tenor and bass sections. He would join in heartily in his deep, mellow bass voice and we must have sounded like a revival meeting in progress at times. This would probably be frowned upon now, if not actually forbidden but I can't tell that it has harmed any of us—quite the opposite, in fact.

He meted out punishment swiftly when needed, although some of his eighth grade boys were nearly as big as he. I can't ever remember of his spanking a girl but a few times someone would have to stand in a corner with their nose to the wall. Most of all, he wanted us to learn.

The love of nature was evident in his life and he taught us many things about the outdoors. When the procession of school children lined up for the field trip, he would put a responsible child in the front of the line and another at the end to "bring up the rear."

He would walk back and forth, showing us different plants and flowers and identifying shrubs and trees. He showed us how to identify the edible meadow mushroom, which he called the "Bradley mushroom," and introduced us to its excellent eating qualities.

Even on our field trips, we couldn't get away from music. As we climbed the steep slope of Pilot Knob, our voices resounded in three-part rounds, one of which went, "We're marching off together/To climb the distant peak/This lovely autumn weather/The mountain top we seek!" Never mind that it was lovely spring weather, we sang just as lustily.

After teaching the same family of youngsters for several years, he became a friend as well as a teacher. Several times we went camping and trout fishing together and I remember how he enjoyed it, as well as the ramps we cooked there.

After he became very ill with cancer, my mother and father went to visit him at his daughter's house. The flesh had melted away on his huge frame but the big wide grin was still the same.

On a spring day such as this, when the daisies are beginning to bloom and Pilot Knob beckons, I think of Mr. Hinkle and the long-ago field trips. I wish I could tell him how he did inspire a love of learning in me and how many things he taught that I still remember. His life made a lasting impact on mine.

I guess I'll pick a bouquet of daisies and let my mind drift back to those old school days that will never be forgotten.

The Charleston Gazette
May 20, 1994

The Clay County Free Press
May 25, 1994

The laundry chores of today bear little resemblance to the wash days of yesterday. In fact, the very term "wash day" is obsolete. We no longer have designated wash days, but it can be "wash nights" or any time that you want to toss a load of clothes in the washer and dryer. We now have convenient little packets of pre-measured detergent and fabric softener that we throw in along with the dirty laundry, push a button, and go on about our business. Sometimes I wonder how we can stay so busy with all these labor-saving devices! I have less time than I used to have when all six kids were at home.

My girls, with their gleaming automatic washers and dryers, would cringe at the wash days of my early marriage.   It was customary to set aside a day in the week, usually Monday, solely for doing laundry. Plans were often made the night before, when the water was carried or drawn from a well by the more able-bodied men in the family. It was a source of pride among the neighborhood women to be the first to get the clean laundry hung out on the clothesline. (It may be just a rumor, but one lady was suspected of doing her laundry the night before, and rising at the crack of dawn in order to be the first to get her clothes on the line. Now that was sneaky!)

In mild weather, I loved doing the laundry. The wash water was heated outside in the "black" tub, which was reserved expressly for that purpose. As soon as breakfast was over, I would build a fire (firewood was collected through the week and piled beside the tub). The creek behind the house ran clear and clean at that time and I would scoop buckets of water and fill the tub. I also remember stepping on an ice-covered rock one cold March day and taking a plunge into that freezing water. This was the good old days?

While the water heated, I would hurriedly do the morning housework. Mom always brought her wash water to a boil, so of course I did too.

Then the hot water was carried and poured into the wringer washer on the back porch (the washing machine reposed in the kitchen during the cold winter months). Soap was added, and the first load of white clothes. I used a cut-off broomstick to lift the wet clothes to feed through the wringer, where they were run through into another tub of hot water in which bleach had been added (When we got to the dark-colored clothes, we skipped the bleach water). After they had soaked for a few minutes, they were put through the wringer again into a tub of cold water colored with a jigger or two of Little Boy Blue blueing. This made the white clothes fairly sparkle in the bright sunshine.

In my mind, I am back at that little house doing laundry again. A warm breeze ruffles the leaves on the big Lombardy poplar tree and I can smell the peculiar fragrance the shiny, sticky leaves exude. It is combined with the odor of crushed peppermint where it has been trodden underfoot along the ditch line. I look up the "little" road and see Criss coming home from visiting Jim and Minnie Butler and I finish hanging the last of Patty's diapers on the line. Can it really be thirty-two(now it is more than forty-three) years ago?

Doing laundry in the winter was a hard chore, no matter how you looked at it. Water was heated on the kitchen cookstove and clothes had to be hung out regardless of the weather. Sometimes they would freeze as you hung them on the line and had to be pried loose when they were dry. It was an all-day job, leaving the housewife exhausted and sometimes cranky. It still wasn't as hard as Mom's washday, however.

I can barely remember her using the time-honored washboard, although she, like all other housewives of that day and time, did all of her laundry bent over that instrument of torture. She still used it after she got the gasoline powered Maytag wringer washer to scrub some of the heavily soiled articles before she added it to the wash. I remember that old Maytag washer well. She used drip gasoline to fuel it and it had a starter that had to be kicked to get it going. It was noisy, and emitted gasoline fumes but it was still much better than that woman-powered washboard.

I am sure that many a knuckle has been sacrificed on that washboard; knuckles that were already softened by homemade lye soap. Before the days of the Maytag, each piece of clothing had to be scrubbed, on the washboard, wrung out by hand and the procedure repeated in the rinse water. There was no "advanced formula" detergents and whiteners either—just homemade lye soap and bars of Fels Naptha. Mom remembers the first box of soap powder that she ever saw, called "Chipso."

There were magazine advertisements when I was old enough to read touting Fels Naptha soap. I remember seeing one that said, "Hate graveyard gray? Chase it away with Fels Naptha soap!" (One time my brother Mark, when he was a little young'en, got into some sort of mischief and Mom gave him a "whuppin." He came through the house crying and with his mouth twisted to one side, he told us, "Don't let that gray, graveyard color fool you—there's plenty of life in the old hag yet!")

Mom's mother had it even worse—they heated their wash water in the winter in the fireplace. I don't know why they didn't use the wood cookstove, unless with all eleven youngsters and three meals a day, they didn't want to tie it up. Mom says that she remembers many times when the "fore stick" would burn in two and the big kettle would tilt over, scattering ashes and water all over the floor. And sometimes we think we have it rough!

The only advantage they had, as far as I can see, is that with a designated washday to do their laundry chores there was a great sense of accomplishment in a completed job. Nevertheless, I think I will gather up a huge load of laundry, throw it in my

automatic washer and thank the good
Lord that Grandma's day is over!

The Clay Herald
February 29, 1988

The Charleston Gazette
May 22, 1992

Our Heavenly Father has opened the
windows of heaven and poured out upon
the hills the blessing of a perfect
spring day. It was spring on the
calendar and spring in the warm breezes
and cloudless blue sky. Winter may
return again with snow flurries and
freezing wind to chill the lilac buds
and halt the shrill song of the spring
peepers. No matter—today we have
spring and she will return.

The windy weather of March always
reminds me of one of my husband's older
brothers, Cornelius. He is gone now, to
a land where heavenly breezes blow but
the family stories about him will live
on for generations.

It was fitting that he was born in
March, for no one could spin out
stories by the hour like Cornelius
could. It was like a family reunion, a
Fourth of July celebration and
Christmas all rolled in one when he
came to visit. Our children would sit
for hours on the edge of their chairs,

204

listening open-mouthed to the tall tales that Uncle Cornelius would spin. He had a special attachment for our daughter Patty, who was born on his March 6 birthday.

He was a big man, tall and broad-shouldered, with a rough, craggy face and large, work-worn hands. He was mostly a coal miner and a farmer, although he had held other occupations. He was a brute of a man, who worked hard and lived hard as well. There was no one just like him and he was well liked by one and all.

He would recall stories about growing up on a rocky, hillside farm in the upper corner of Clay County, laughing over hard times and Depression days. One of my favorite stories concerned Cornelius and the dead horse.

Cornelius was the second oldest son in a family of nine children and like most large families of that time, it was a backbreaking job to eke out a living on a hillside farm. One of their greatest possessions was a work horse named Old Prince.

Cornelius' father, called "Poppy" by all of his children, was especially proud of Old Prince. One hot summer day, Poppy and the boys were putting up oats. Old Prince was balky that day for some reason and Poppy had his patience sorely tried by the shenanigans of the horse. In a fit of irritation, Poppy thundered, "When we get these oats up, I hope you drop dead!"

As fate would have it, when the last bundle of oats was gathered up, the old horse fell right down in the traces and gave up the ghost. Poppy was flabbergasted, to say the least. Criss says he remembers Cornelius coming to the house that evening with the harness draped over his shoulders, kicking and squealing like a horse (behind Poppy's back, of course).

It was late evening, so they decided to wait until the following day to bury Old Prince. It was a hot summer night and the next morning they found the poor horse swollen to twice his normal size. Prince had to have a proper burial, however, so Poppy and the boys dug and dug.

Cornelius got tired of fooling with it, so he caught Poppy's back turned and cut the horse's legs off. Just as Poppy turned around, speechless at the desecration of his animal, Cornelius r'ared back and sunk the double-bitted ax deep in the horse's bloated side. There was no use to run for the hills—it was too late. "It's easier to make the horse fit the hole, than to make the hole fit the horse," Cornelius explained. Years later, Poppy related the story to us. He could finally laugh about it.

One year, Patty got her Uncle Cornelius a birthday card that had the picture of a horse on the front of it. When she got home, she discovered that the envelope was too small for the card. She had to cut the card off to make it fit the envelope, and inside she wrote him a little note beginning, "One time I heard about a man who had to make a horse fit a hole ... "

Poppy's family and a neighbor family used to trade work, helping each other put up hay and hoe corn. The younger children took turns carrying drinking water to the workers, who were toiling in the hot sunshine high on their river ridge farms. One blistering day one of the neighbor children brought a bucket of cold water to the thirsty workers. They passed the bucket around thankfully and just as the last person was assuaging his thirst, Doris piped up, "Don't drink all that water—my pet turtle is in the bottom of it!"

The Charleston Gazette
March 25, 1994

The Clay County Free Press
March 30, 1994

St. Patrick's Day unfurled gloomy and cloudy, without any "wearin' of the green" on the hills. Pillars of dirty snow stand along the roadside, a grotesque monument to last week's blizzard. Paw Braley invariably planted his potatoes on St. Patrick's Day, come rain or shine. He would have been hard put to get them in the ground this year.

I hope that our descriptive, flavorful mountain dialect never dies out. It is as salty as a churn of pickled corn and as full-bodied as a cup of hot sassafras tea that has been brewed until it is rich and red.

Although we unconsciously use many of the words and phrases that our parents and grandparents used, I am afraid that much of it has already been watered down. Even so, I have noticed many people trying to suppress a grin when I am talking. I asked my friend Neva if people are laughing at me and being a hillbilly herself, she assured me that they were not. We can laugh at ourselves and laugh with others but mountain people resent being laughed at—especially by outsiders.

I reckon I've heard my husband use this phrase hundreds of times during our marriage but for some reason it stuck out to me when he repeated it a few days ago. "I ain't got 'ary a boy that can keep up with me working," he lamented. My dad would have said, "I ain't got nary a boy . . ."

Then later, Criss made the comment about a certain member of our family, "She's a right smart of a talker." I got to thinking about how many old words and phrases we still use today that would sound strange to someone outside our hills and yet they are second nature to us.

Many of these are pure "Old English," and others came from our Irish and Scottish ancestors. When Criss comes in from work, "he's tired to the bone." Daddy was "plumb wore out," while my mother-in-law, Peach, was "just tuckered out." Grandma O'Dell was, "plumb petered out," which is more descriptive than plain exhausted.

If you were sick, you were "feelin' porely," but when you began to recover, you felt "right peart." "Peart" was also used (and still is) to describe how someone had talked smart to you, such as, "She really pearted me off when I asked her." People who had an exalted opinion of themselves were called "briggity." Briggity-britches was an epithet we hurled at one another when we were children.

Grandma may have gone in the kitchen to cook and found that she didn't have a "haet" of anything to fix—she'd "clean forgot" to go to the garden. If the "sweet milk" wasn't "blinky" she could "bile up" some cornmeal mush. If you were visiting, you were always asked to share a meal, "Take a 'cheer' and set your feet under the table." The polite response to, "Do you want another helpin'?" was "I don't keer." That didn't mean you didn't want it—quite the opposite. Old folks were "clever" when it came to hospitality.

Grandpa might fuss at how us "young'ens" had "clumb" up on the barn roof and warn us that he had "seed" a snake "quiled up" in the weeds in the barnyard and it could have been "p'izen." Grandma would "redd up" the kitchen after the meal. She had a "hard girl" to help with the housework after she got older, but might have to "get shet of" one that wouldn't work. The "pore" girl would put her clothes in a "poke" and head on down the road.

My sister-in-law told me one time that her son had come to visit her one day and he didn't realize that it was her birthday. She said that she didn't "name it to him." I 'low she was hurt, but she didn't "let on" that she was.

When we were kids, we used to torment one another until someone got "worped" around the head. Daddy would have to put a "quietus" on the fussing. Children were different then, as they were expected to be seen and not heard, especially at mealtime and when company came. A cardinal sin in Poppy Bragg's book was for a child to "walk before folks." If you were trapped in a room when they had visitors and the only exit was to walk in front of them where they were seated, you either stayed put or climbed out a back window.

My daughter-in-law, Sarah, once threw me for a loop when she described someone as being "hojous." It took me a while to figure out that she meant hideous. Well, we still say "tejous" for tedious. Last night I caught myself using the word "juberous", which is a

word we commonly use. It finally dawned
on me that it came from "dubious."

I have a friend who writes about
her "grandchurn." I related this to Mom
and she recalled the flower bush that
her mother had in the front yard when
she was a child. She called it a "Rosy
Churn," and Mom suddenly realized that
it was a Rose of Sharon bush!

The Charleston Gazette
March 26, 1993

A lone swallowtail butterfly
hovers lightly over a bright yellow
clump of evening primroses, unhurriedly
tasting the sweet nectar. He seems to
have all the time in the world but in
the cicada's strident cry there is
injected an urgent note. The rasping,
mournful cry of the katydid is heard
louder each night, warning us that
summer is dying and autumn is coming
soon. The early morning mist covers the
hills and lingers later each day, while
the grass and trees have a tired, weary
look. My father always told us that
after the katydid's first cry, it would
be six weeks until frost.

Late summer flowers are blooming
now, tall purple ironweed appearing in
fields and meadows and the true
harbinger of autumn, yellow sprays of
goldenrod. Green thimbles form on the

thimbleweed where the little white flowers previously bloomed, while through the fuzzy leaves of the mullein a tall stalk of yellow blossoms pushes its way upward. The towering mauve blossoms of Joe-Pye weed are in full bloom and along the roadbanks the underbrush is beginning to redden. Summer is on the wane.

The grandchildren try frantically to cram their last week of vacation full of activities. All too soon for them, the gates of freedom will slam shut with the coming of the yellow school bus. I remember trying to wring out the last bit of play from summer.

When I was a little girl, the word "fairy" conjured up visions of tiny, ethereal creatures dressed in billowing, gossamer gowns, who sneaked out by night and danced in the moonlight. We believed in them. Oh, we really knew better, but it was such fun to imagine that these little beings really existed. I remember how enchanted I was when I read "Peter Pan." As well as I can remember, the book stated, "When the very first baby laughed its very first laugh, it broke up into a million pieces and began skipping around. These were the first fairies. And every time a child states, 'I don't believe in fairies,' somewhere in the world a fairy dies." We didn't permit anyone in our presence to make such a statement.

On long golden summer days, making fairy houses was one of our favorite activities. We weren't allowed to play in the "big road," where traffic whizzed back and forth, but the "little road" that ran right beside our house seldom had a car on it. The dirt bank above the road was yellow clay, and easy to hollow out into rectangular cubicles. After the house was square and smooth enough to suit us, then came the delightful task of furnishing it. We were always on the lookout for miniature objects that we could use in our fairy houses. As we worked, we talked among ourselves, "I wonder if the fairies would like this?" we would ask, holding up a fancy button. Or, "Won't they be surprised when they find this in their house?"

We would use penny matchboxes to make beds, with the coverlet fashioned from a fuzzy mullein leaf. We made tiny tables and set them with acorn cups and wee bouquets of miniscule wild flowers. Oh, the happy hours we whiled away letting our imaginations run rampant!

While we didn't have a lot of "bought" toys, we made up for it by pretending. Sometimes Mary Ellen would find a fancy button or a shiny rhinestone from a lapel pin and I would tell her to lay it on the floor of the fairy house where they would find it. Then I would sneak out and pin it on the wall with a long thorn and let her find it the next day. "Oh, look what the fairies did with your button," I would cry in feigned surprise. Of course she knew better but it was such fun to pretend.

Summers seemed long and magical when I was a child. We got up each morning with the thrill of "no school today." We filled our playtime with imaginative activities and I never remember being bored or having nothing to do.

There was the barn, with its mounds of sweet-smelling hay. We were forbidden to romp in it, which made it more fun. But sometimes we would simply lie around in it, discussing what we were going to be "when we grew up." I wonder if any of us fulfilled our childhood daydreams.

When we roamed the woods, we kept an eye out for a location to make another playhouse. Sometimes we would find flat, mossy rocks with a ring of mushrooms nearby. Of course, it was a fairy ring and you could see where they had been dancing in the moonlight! There we would make fairy hats. All we needed was a variety of leaves, a handful of thorns from a thorn apple bush, some wild flowers and our imaginations. Fifth Avenue has never come up with the winsome creations we designed. We would leave row upon row of lovely, flower bedecked hats on the mossy rock. We could imagine the delighted surprise when the fairies

came out to dance that night and found
our offering.

Children today are exposed much too
early to the harsh, brutal realities of
life. My young grandchildren are more
aware of certain social evils than when
I was an older teenager. I liked it
better when "fairies" meant miniature
houses in the road-bank and an
enchanted summer of fun.

The Charleston Gazette
September 4, 1992

CHAPTER EIGHT

THE WILD SIDE OF THE HILLS

"What is a weed? A plant
whose virtues have not
yet been discovered."
...Ralph Waldo Emerson

Spring peeps shyly around the corner of April as if wondering whether to come on in or let winter have the stage a little longer. The voice of the spring peepers is heard in the land, coaxing her to come forward in all her beauty.

She has sent forerunners ahead with a liberal sprinkling of snowdrops, daffodils and hyacinths. Tiny yellow crocuses compete with the wild coltsfoot for brightness, while buds are swelling on the lilacs and apple trees. There is a greenish-yellow glow about the weeping willow tree, as if it can't wait to shoot forth its leaves. The air is milder now but the green tears of spring keep falling.

After the warm, spring-like weather of January, March came in as a shock with its bitter dose of true wintertime. We are all ready for spring to come. There is time to dig some more sassafras roots, and we just received our first mess of ramps. Soon the morel mushrooms will be popping their wrinkled heads through the rich humus of the woodlands. We await eagerly each spring for the appearance of these gourmet-fare mushrooms that are worth the hours of searching that it sometimes takes. They have an exquisite flavor, and I like them best simply sautéed in a little butter or bacon grease. Some people roll them in flour and fry them in hot butter or oil but I think that the flour masks the flavor. We have used them in spaghetti and pizza and chopped in gravy. It seems a waste to mix them with other foods, when they are so good by themselves.

Ramps can be prepared in a variety of ways, although we like ours chopped and simmered for a few minutes in bacon grease (with the crumbled bacon added to it) and then beaten eggs are added to the whole mess. They are good fried with potatoes and some like them merely stewed like greens. Spring is hardly complete without a good mess of ramps and we usually indulge in them during our first fishing and camping trip of the season. They seem to go along with fried trout and corn bread.

Nature offers us so many wild foods in the spring. Dandelion greens, while they are young and tender, are a tasty food to add to the dinner menu. They should be gathered before the first buds appear on them and can be used raw with a boiled dressing made with milk, vinegar, eggs and sugar. I like them added to mixed wild green and cooked tender.

My favorite wild greens, however, are poke greens. They are best when they first come through the ground, pink and tender. I parboil them for a few minutes, drain the water and add fresh water to finish cooking them. These are good simply buttered as you would broccoli or asparagus. My sister-in-law, Alice, always cooked equal proportions of poke stalks and milkweed, but I like poke by itself.

There are many wild greens that I have never tried, although they are there for the taking. Last spring I cooked cleavers, or goosegrass, for the first time and it was delicious. According to old herbal books, this herb is supposed to be helpful in shedding the excess poundage that winter diets seem to add. According to herbal lore, if it is cooked in mutton broth, with or without oatmeal, it will "keepe them leane and lanke that are apt to grow fatte." I am sorry to report that it didn't work for me. It must have been the lack of mutton broth—it couldn't have been the skillet of corn bread slathered with butter that I ate with it.

These wild greens are rich in vitamins and minerals and have a medicinal value as well as being tasty. Wintercress, nettles and violet leaves are exceptionally high in Vitamin A and violet leaves are far richer in Vitamin C than any other leafy vegetable.

This year I plan to try a couple of new things. One is dandelion buds, which should be gathered any time now. You are supposed to dig up the plants, open them up and take out the tiny, new buds that would eventually develop into mature blossoms. They are white on the outside and pale yellow on the inside.

They are boiled for just a few minutes
and then seasoned with butter, salt and
pepper. They are supposed to taste like
artichoke hearts. I am afraid it will
take days to gather enough for one
mess.

Another wild food that I have
always planned to try is purslane
greens. They grow rampant in our garden
during the summer and we used to pull
bushels of this weed for our pigs.
Grandma O'Dell used to cook this for a
vegetable, although that was before my
time.

You are supposed to pick these
before the seed appears in the top
(this plant has a little yellow flower)
and cook it while it is still tender.
Wash and cook in a small amount of
water, as you would spinach, for only a
few minutes. Seasoned with bacon
grease or butter, it is supposed to be
quite tasty and loaded with vitamins.

Although the mist is hanging over
Pilot Knob and the day is gloomy and
cloudy, the grass has turned a vibrant
green after two days of sunshine last
week. April comes, and with her plenty
of wild foods to enjoy. I can hardly
wait.

The Charleston Gazette
April 2, 1993

The woods and hillsides are
beginning to abound with many of the

wild delicacies that spring has to offer the residents of our hills. From the lowly ramp, whose voice speaks in robust tones, to the tiny wild mushrooms that are hidden among the dead leaves on the forest floor, the woods are full of good things to eat.

A hearty ramp dinner is as necessary to springtime as sassafras tea and will tone a sluggish system dulled by wintertime. After a good mess of ramps, a person is ready to face the many chores that warm weather brings and will give a spirited and energetic outlook on life. I feel ready for summer.

Avid mushroom hunters are scouring the hills for the morel mushroom now, probably the most-prized specimen that grows in our area. They are called by many common names, such as "Molly moochers," or "muggles." We have always called them "merkles," but whatever you call them, they are plain delicious. When our pastor first moved to these hills, just a green boy fresh from the streets of Baltimore, one of the men in the congregation asked him if he wanted to go merkle hunting. With a puzzled look on his face he replied, "Well, I don't have a gun!"

It may not take a gun, but it does take a sharp eye and a lot of grit and patience to comb the woods for these elusive fungi. Regular hunters have their territory staked out from year to year and are more secretive about their morel patches than they are their bank accounts.

The morel mushroom is spread by spores and can generally be found in the same area year after year. The half-free morel, which is the one that is appearing now in damp, open woods, is often found around beech, oak and poplar trees. They are yellow-brown in color, turning darker with age and have a honeycombed cap on a whitish stalk. They blend in so well with the dead, brown leaves of last fall that they are sometimes hard to spot.

The yellow morel, which appears seven to ten days later than the half-free, is our favorite. It is called the "honeycomb morel," and when it has white ribs and grayish pits, it is called the "white morel." This succulent morsel is found many times in old fruit orchards, growing around apple, cherry and pear trees. They, too, grow around poplar trees and dead leaves and I have even found them around old fence posts. Sometimes they come up in burned-out areas, such as where brush piles have been burned. Once a person becomes familiar with these morels, they are easy to identify.

There is a poisonous morel called the "false morel" that we run across occasionally, but it is easy to distinguish by splitting it open. The inside is chambered whereas the edible morel is hollow. Also, the false morel is squatty and thick, with a brain-like head on a short thick stalk. With a good mushroom guide and a little comparison, it shouldn't be hard to learn to differentiate between the two.

I have read that mushrooms should not be soaked in water (and this is true of the oyster mushroom) but merely wiped clean with a damp paper towel. The wild morel must be soaked. We split the little fellows, wash them through several changes of water, and then soak them overnight in salt water. There is a minuscule "bug" that infests morels, and will float on top of the water. I have a feeling that we may have eaten more than one of these varmints, but a bug that likes merkles can't be all bad.

Morels can be cooked in a variety of ways, but the way we like them best is to drain well, then simply sauté them in a little butter or bacon grease. They can be rolled in flour and fried, or used in a variety of recipes. Any way that you fix them, they are good.

One year we gathered more than we could use, so I froze a few bags of them. I thought it affected the flavor and the texture. This year my brother told me to cover them with water and freeze them—so far, we haven't found that many yet.

For the next two or three weeks, the yellow morel mushrooms will be popping up through the ground, just

waiting for someone to grab them and
carry them away. Even if you only find
a few or none at all, it is a rewarding
experience to roam through the hills in
springtime. God walks these hills in
the spring and one can feel His
presence all around.

The Charleston Gazette
April 22, 1994

The Clay County Free Press
April 27, 1994

Summer has ended. The first week of
autumn dissolves into bright sunshine
and blue skies, with puffy, white
clouds overlooking the earth below.
They move lazily across the sky,
creating dappled shadows that march
slowly across the hilltops and drape
the hollows in patches of darkness.

The recent rains have washed the
wooded slopes clean of the dust and
dryness of the drought and injected new
life into the tired and weary leaves.
Their fresh, green color glistens in
the warm sunshine, but it will be
short-lived. Autumn is an aging beauty
struggling valiantly to retain her
youth but the dyed roots of her hair
are growing out. Among the green of her
hills, the autumn hues of yellow and
bronze are showing.

225

She is decking herself out in the brilliant colors of autumn, with lavish displays of gold, purple, yellow and blue. On her brow she wears the goldenrod's pure gold and she is robed in the regal purple of the ironweed. The wild asters drop their blue-fringed eyes as she passes by and the touch-me-not offers orange jewels for her adorning. She is scented with the light fragrance of the evening primrose, mixed with the warm, earthy perfume of rich soil and ripening nuts.

Autumn is a lady of many moods. She can be warm, bright and inviting as she is today, or change quickly into a dark, lowering day. She is subject to fits of melancholia, with gloom and sadness marring her brow. She seems to sense that her reign is short, with cold winter hard on her heels and his chilly breath on the back of her neck.

In spite of her changing moods, or perhaps because of them, fall is my favorite of all the seasons. She is free and lavish with her rich gifts, reaching out with a generous hand to those who take advantage of her bounty. The tender, tasty meadow mushrooms are popping up overnight in the mowed grass beside the garden, ready to be gathered each morning. Two of the grandsons, Adrian and Joseph, brought in a large paper bag full of the sulphur shelf mushroom, also called the "chicken mushroom." To me, this is one of the most delicious edible mushrooms in our area. This was growing on the side of a dead tree and was fresh and tender.

This mushroom grows in overlapping clusters, with red-orange on top and with bright yellow underneath. I cut the woody stem away where it had been attached to the tree, then sliced it thin, rolled it in flour and fried it in bacon grease (Yes, bacon grease—there are some things that really cry out for it) I had a whole gang of kids and grandkids in that day and we had a feast. This mushroom can vary in color, from salmon to sulphur-yellow or bright orange. It must be picked while very young and tender, as it hardens with age and becomes indigestible.

As Criss was enjoying his tasty "chicken" on a homemade, hot biscuit, he remarked, "Think of how many people miss out on delicious food like this simply because they won't try it." I am quite cautious of trying out any new variety of mushroom unless I am really sure that it is edible. If I can't definitely identify it, I leave it alone. Mom picked a large handful of chanterelle mushrooms that were growing under her pine trees and brought them to me awhile back. She told me that she thought they were chanterelles but I had left my mushroom guide at Beckley and wasn't sure of them. I found out later that the chanterelle mushroom is probably the most prized and popular mushroom in the world. They were chanterelles and I will latch on to the next ones.

Son Andy brought home a load of ripe pawpaws last week. He had taken his coat off and tied the sleeves to make a pouch to carry them(Patty still laughs about the two little boys in grade school who brought ripe pawpaws to school for a snack and stored them in the pocket of their pants). I relish them, but some people can't stand them. It is hard to be indifferent about a pawpaw—you either like them or you don't.

I froze some of the pulp, after seeding and peeling them, to make a pawpaw pie later. My sister, Mary Ellen, makes a lovely pawpaw cake. There are many good things waiting to be gathered. The butternuts are falling from Andy's trees, and Criss reports that there is a bumper crop of wild grapes in the woods. I want to mix some apple and wild grape juice for jelly and hunt some persimmons after it has frosted.

Summer is ended, but the harvest goes on.

The Charleston Gazette
September 29, 1995

The Clay County Free Press
October 4, 1995

CHAPTER NINE

GOING BACK HOME AGAIN

> "Things bygone are the only things
> that last:
> The present is mere grass, quick-
> mown away;
> The past is stone, and stands for
> ever fast."
>
> ...Eugene Lee-Hamilton

Today I looked at my younger sister and a middle-aged lady stared back at me. Oh, Mary Ellen, where did yesterday go?

It was only yesterday that Mom's young fingers were firmly braiding our hair, ironing our dresses and tying up our sore toes.' How bright the memories, how near the past is linked with this warm summer night . . .

Good old summertime, running after dark . . . dress sashes flying as we catch lightning bugs rising up from the wet grass . . . delicious scream of terror as we dodge the unexpected hop toad that is intent on catching his own insects. Forever we were running . . . leaping into the sudden, buoyant wind that sprung up right before a thunderstorm . . . cavorting like gazelles on the wings of the wind.

Where are the games of yesterday, Mary Ellen? "Bushel of wheat/bushel of clover/who's not ready can't hide over. I'm comin'!" . . . "Wire, brier, limber-lock/three geese in a flock/one flew east, one flew west/one flew over the cuckoo's nest—O-U-T spells out goes he!" . . . "My chickie, my chickie/my craney, my crow/went to the well/to wash his big toe/when he got back/his black hen was gone/what time is it, old witch?" . . . "Who's going 'round my house this dark stormy night? . . . Old Bloody Butcher!". .

They are gone and barely remembered.

And the children who ran and played on the Virginia office porch—where are they? Gone forever, some of them—Cody and Alen Wayne, Betty Marie and Avis, Bill and Dud . . . and Mark. And the others? Scattered here and there . . . Florida and Maine, Texas, California and New York . . . Those scattered ones, do they ever think of yesterday, and the hills of home?

Remember the work of yesterday, Mary Ellen? Was the sun hotter, or did it just seem so? Picking up those endless rocks out of the garden that the winter seemed to spawn each spring. Sweat bees and chiggers and sand briers that attacked our bare feet . . . blackberries ripe and mornings cool . . . hot, hot afternoons and more sweat bees . . . purple-smeared mouths and spilled buckets of berries . . . long rows of corn . . . hoeing, hoeing, hoeing . . . blessed relief on a rainy day. . . yes, they are gone . . . those hot days of toil.

The days of innocent play are gone also, Mary Ellen. Sleepy Holler and long hours of "Let's play like" . . . our own private refuge from the world of adults . . . spurred blue violets and wild irises populated our world . . . moss and ferns and smell of rich earth . . . the enormous log that spanned the holler, dwarfing two little girls . . . mud cakes and Mason jar lid dishes . . . pretend and pure joy.

The food of yesterday, where is it? Wild strawberries, wee pointed ones, sweet as honey on the tongue . . . Peppermint and sour grass, sweet birch and mountain tea . . . sassafras sprouts, tender and crunchy . . . dewberries and blackberries warmed by the sun.

The food that Mom cooked—nothing has ever tasted so good since . . . slumgullion made from yesterday's leftovers . . . with a chopped onion and a quart of home-canned tomatoes added to the skillet . . . warm cottage cheese, freshly made . . . creamed new potatoes and peas . . . hot corn bread, brown and crusty from the iron skillet . . . leaf lettuce and tender green onions dressed in bacon grease and vinegar . . . food doesn't taste like that now.

Mary Ellen, where did the security go? That blessed, peaceful bedtime, when we lay down at night and knew that whatever happened, Mommy and Daddy would take care of it . . . sleep undisturbed by worries and cares . . . two big beds and four little girls. . . shared secrets and warm love . . .

Where are those little babies that we sung to . . . told endless stories to . . . watched and protected? Are they still waiting somewhere in the past, waiting for "Go to sleep, my little buckaroo," one more time?

Mary Ellen, where did our childhood go—so fast?

The Charleston Gazette
July 8, 1994

The Clay County Free Press
July 13, 1994

The spray of goldenrod that bloomed cheerily from the vase in the kitchen window has turned gray and fuzzy and the twig of sourwood that accompanied it is now bare. It once flaunted bright red leaves and now they lie on the windowsill, crisp and dark. It is an echo of the view through the window, where the former beauty of autumn has fallen under a sudden attack of wintery weather.

Patches of wet snow glaze the fallen leaves on the hillsides and the grassy areas are encrusted with the same. Cold wind has replaced the balmy breezes of a few days ago and Indian summer is an unrealized dream. She is a shy maiden who may, or may not, appear this year.

With the holiday season looming closer, many folks are making plans to go home again. "Going home again" is an urgent need deep in the heart of most of us, and the anticipation brings a warm and tender feeling. Although I have never traveled far, or for very long from the family fold, there have been times in my life when being away from home brought on a terrible bout of homesickness.

When Criss and I first married and moved out of state, it was quite difficult to adjust to being away from my parents. Many times throughout the day, I needed to ask Mom's advice about something and she wasn't there. It was a panicky feeling to be on your own and home seemed so far away. I missed the companionship at night, when we all gathered together to discuss the events of the day. I don't think a person appreciates the security and safety of a happy home, with godly parents who provide everything we need, until we begin one of our own. There were times when I longed to be a little girl again with no adult decisions to be made.

Our oldest daughter, Patty, has lived most of her married life only a stone's throw from us. I remember how I grieved when she first married, telling Criss that home would never be the same with Patty gone. I was so depressed the next morning that Criss took me to visit Aunt Eva, just to get my mind off Patty's leaving. When we came back home and pulled into the driveway, Patty was sweeping the front porch. That has been a symbol of our life. She has been there for us as well.

A few years ago, her husband secured employment near Elyria, Ohio and moved the family there. It was a grievous ordeal for Patty. Every day she mourned the fact that her heart was here in the hills. It got so bad that Randy had to move her back home.

Like many others, my old home is gone, at lest as far as the building is concerned. When I think about going home again, Grandpa is there in his rocking chair, with the newest baby on his lap. Mom is doing some of the unending mending, probably patching the torn knees of the boys' overalls, while Daddy is reading to us. It is night and the gas flame leaps high in the heating stove, it is cold and snowy outside.

Daddy is reading to us the story of Joseph, the little Israelite boy who was sold into slavery and taken far from home and we are deeply engrossed in it. Then we are all kneeling along the couch and beside our chairs while Daddy prays and asks God to bless and keep each one of us. There is love and security in that old house.

Yes, you can go home again. As long as memory lasts, the loved ones at home are waiting there in the recesses of the mind, to comfort and encourage the heart. Mom told me one time that she thought heaven would be like going back home again, back to her old home place on the banks of Big Laurel Creek. Dad and Maw would be there and all of her brothers and sisters, secure and warm in the family love that surrounded them. She could be right. How could heaven be any better than going home again?

The Charleston Gazette
November 17, 1995

The Clay County Free Press
November 22, 1995

Just one more time, I'd like to go back home for Christmas.

I'd like to climb on the wooden sled with Larry and let Daddy pull us across the snow to hunt for the perfect pine tree. The air would be crisp and exhilarating and the snow would crunch underfoot as Daddy pulled the sled across the crusty surface.

We would search carefully for just the right tree. It had to be a short-needled pine for fragrance and it had to be tall enough to touch the nine-foot ceiling in the front room. There would be deep pockets of snow in the shady hollow and Daddy's gumboots would almost disappear as he searched. Finally with cold hands and red cheeks, we would find one that suited Daddy and we would load it on the sled.

I'd like to run back into the old house once again, where the welcome heat would meet us as we opened the front door. The gas stove would be turned up high, flames licking above the top of the stove. Shedding our coats and boots, we would run to the stove to soak up the life-giving heat.

Mom would be in the kitchen and mouth-watering smells would taunt our appetites. Cinnamon-rich fragrance of apple pies would be wafting from the oven and she would be garnishing the orange-coconut cake with a liberal sprinkling of shredded coconut over the snowy white icing. Mark and Ronnie would be standing in line to "lick the bowls," while Mom stirred the homemade butterscotch filling for yet more pies.

How I'd like to walk down the old dirt road, snow-covered and white, to take part in the Hagar School program. The night would be clear and icy cold and a million stars would twinkle in the black velvet sky. We would look for one particularly bright star and wonder if it were the same star that shone over Bethlehem and guided the wise men to find Jesus. Excitement would course through our whole being like Fourth of July sparklers, as we anticipated our parts in the Christmas program.

Most of all, I would like to gather around Mom and Daddy at night, while Daddy read the story of Jesus' birth from the Bible. I can hear his voice now, tender and compassionate, as he explained how Mary and Joseph were turned away from the inn and took refuge in a lowly stable.

As we would kneel to pray in the big front room, we could almost hear the heavenly chorus of the angels

ringing in our ears as they rejoiced in
the birth of our Savior. Daddy's humble
prayer would echo their thanksgiving,
as he would thank the Lord for God's
greatest gift of love.

The years have rolled on and many
things have changed. The past will
never change and precious memories
linger on down through the years.

The Charleston Gazette
December 13, 1996

The Clay County Free Press
December 18, 1996

AFTERWARD

Since I began writing these columns, more than eighteen years ago, there have been many, many changes in our world, our nation and our own family.

Life flows on like a river—sometimes placidly, sometimes with unexpected twists and curves. There are hidden dangers, submerged logs and tricky currents. We never know what lies around the bend in the river . . .

The little ones I began writing about are grown now, with families of their own.

Michael's children, Jeremy, David and Christina, are young adults; none of them married, except Jeremy is "promised."

Patty's Aaron is married and they are expecting their first baby in December. This will be our third great-grandchild. Luke and Adrian are still at home.

Kevin's Joshua is married and the father of two little girls, Morgan and Molly, barely a year apart. He lives in sight of us, in my late brother Mark's house. Abigail has a serious suitor and Rueben, at eight years of age, still travels across the driveway and spends time with his Poppaw and Mommaw.

Andy's older children are about grown also; Benji has made his home with us for the past two years. Jessica has been accepted into West Virginia Institution of Technology's School of Nursing this fall, and Joseph is in high school. His two little ones, Nicholas and baby Taylor, live right beside us and bring a lot of joy into our lives.

Matthew married his high school sweetheart, Tammy, and they have four little girls: Megan, Judy (Alexandria), Rachel, and baby Belinda. They, too, live very close to us.

Crystal and her husband live in the mountains of North Carolina. They have two little girls, Alyssa and Brionna, who are trying to grow hair for Crystal to experiment with.

If time lasts, there will be many more changes. Perhaps it is one of the stages of growing older that makes a person think about death. I tried to explain my feelings to Matthew one time as we were driving down an interstate highway. Just as we topped a hill, a lonely, wind-swept cemetery came into view—a small, enclosed plot of land studded with tombstones and circled by cedar trees. The sight of one of these hilltop graveyards stirs unnamed feelings deep within my being.

"That's what we are all coming to, Matthew," I began as he shot me an apprehensive look. I continued, "If I were to die right now, I'm sure you kids would miss me terribly. And the older grandchildren would feel a great loss. But to the younger ones, and the unborn ones, my memory would be kept alive only by the things the older ones told them. Then another generation would say, 'I had a great-grandmother who liked to write and who was a bit weird.' A generation later, I would be forgotten, and be just another tombstone on a lonely hillside." Matthew muttered, "Mom, you are weird!"

I'm so glad that is not all there is to it, however. The Apostle Paul stated, "If in this life only we have hope, we are of all men most miserable." Thank God for this hope that is an anchor to the soul.

To God, we are more than a forgotten tombstone—when we receive salvation, we receive eternal life. I have this assurance that if I continue to live faithful to Him, when this life is over, I can go back home again—eternally.

THE END